HOW I LEARNED TO
ROCK MY LIFE

HOW I LEARNED TO ROCK MY LIFE

The Peter Dankelson Story

PETER DANKELSON AND
DEDE DANKELSON

Pete's Diary LLC

First Printing, 2022
Cover Photo - Images by Marie Moore
Cover Design - Dede Dankelson
Interior Formatting - Dede Dankelson
Editing - Megan Eddy
Publishing Consultant - Billy Henrickle

DEDICATION

To Mom, Dad, and Jacob
for your unconditional love and support
Love you always, Peter

To Darin, Jacob, and Peter
my greatest blessings
Dede

Foreword

Peter is a hero of mine. I've known him for some time now. We've met on three different occasions: first in 2008, then in 2013, and finally in 2018. I can honestly say that after each meeting, I felt truly inspired. He's an impressive and charismatic young man. The massive and unique challenge he's been confronted with, having Goldenhar syndrome, would break most of us. Not Peter. His story is one of courage, resilience, and maximizing potential when the odds are seemingly stacked against you.

In this book, you will come to know the attitude, spirit, and wisdom of a true difference maker. Difference makers don't let situation and circumstance define who they are or what they can accomplish. Being a difference maker is a decision to maximize your potential to benefit both yourself and those around you.

It's interesting that when we think about difference makers, we often think about people in sports or business. Peter has found a way to be a difference maker on a different level. He's a difference maker in life and how he lives every day. Reading about how he does it serves as motivation for all of us; anybody looking to maximize their potential, accomplish what others believe impossible, and find the joy in that kind of journey will get something out of this book. It's a must read for those who want to be the best version of themselves – no matter the odds or obstacles.

Peter's self-awareness, positivity and faith is off the charts. What you won't read in this book is a lot of blaming, complaining, or playing the victim. Peter is a role model. He is a young man with a lot of wisdom to share. Peter found a way to maximize what the good Lord gave him. He's done this with the unwavering love and support of his family (even his dogs!) and the help of many doctors and health professionals. His family's love is the gold medal standard. The grind of finding the best science, the best doctors --during surgery and rehab-- is unrelenting. Peter, and his family, can clearly grind with the best of them. These people are special. And so is their story.

I'm humbled by Peter's attitude and accomplishments. His ability to feel great about himself, his life, and his future is something we can all learn from. His courage, his wisdom in focusing on what he can control, and his sense of humor in the face of relentless obstacles serves as an example to all. His willingness to share his journey is a gift. He is a world class energy giver. One of the great passages in this book is, "Kindness is not passive. Being kind means you have the courage to stand up for others. Confident kids can do that. They don't succumb as easily to peer pressure." What a message, especially in today's world.

It becomes clear as we follow Peter throughout his journey, that being a difference maker starts with your mindset. There are many great nuggets of wisdom in his book, including, "Being your own hero starts with being kind to yourself" and "Staying positive during tough times builds your mental grit.

You know that little voice inside your head? It can either build you up or tear you down." You might expect these thoughts from an older person, toward the end of a life well-lived. Not from someone so young.

Peter's intuitive understanding of the aspects and importance of mental health leaves me in awe. It's so common sensical, yet so insightful and real. It's a great message for the youth of the world, and for all of us for that matter. This book will genuinely make you want to be a better human being, which makes it a rare read. And Peter, an even more rare human being.

Mike Babcock
NHL Head Coach, 2002-2019
Stanley Cup Champion, 2008
Olympic Gold Medals, 2010 & 2014

Coach Babcock with the NHL Stanley Cup and the Dankelson Family at Children's Hospital of Michigan
Detroit, 2008

Prologue

When Peter was born with a craniofacial syndrome, my first concern was for his health, but it was quickly followed by my fear for his future. I spent hours at his hospital bedside worrying if he would one day have friends, if he would be bullied in school, and how we would handle the staring.

Never in my wildest dreams did I envision him speaking to hundreds of students about the importance of choosing kindness. Never did I think people would want their picture taken with him or ask for his autograph. Never did I imagine he would be on stage with famous musicians. Being Peter's Mom, however, led me down a road no one could've predicted.

All of those things happened. They happened in Peter's first twenty-one years while undergoing thirty-six surgeries. They happened because he chose courage over fear. That courage created opportunities I couldn't envision when he was born. I was overwhelmed with despair. That's what depression does; it disables your ability to see possibility.

Peter's early years had me in a constant state of grief and anxiety. I viewed myself as a victim of circumstance. I felt trapped and was angry. I was frozen with fear.

Overcoming depression is challenging. No one but you can do the mental and emotional work it takes to work through it. Having a support system, however, is critical to success. My husband found help for me when the grief and anxiety became too much. Darin made sure I had the time and space to do the work. It was a painful and challenging time for us, and I'm proud of how we navigated it together.

Something else that stands out is when we took Peter to meet Coach Mike Babcock before a Detroit Red Wings game. We were sitting in Babcock's office, minutes before the puck drop, as I watched Coach give eight-year-old Peter his full attention. Babcock encouraged Peter to battle his medical issues. He also told him he could be a difference maker. Peter was too young to understand, but it resonated with me.

After working through the mental health issues, I was ready to hear that message. It pushed me to stop wishing things were different. I began thinking more about others and less about my own situation. I stopped being angry and started being grateful. I started thinking about how I could do a better job at playing the cards I was dealt. That's the beginning of Pete's Diary. It's what evolved from my darkest days. It's my commitment to being a difference maker.

Writing and speaking is how I chose to make an impact. I was asked to speak at hospitals about my experience as a parent. When Peter was old enough, I included him in the presentations. Teachers invited us to speak to their classrooms about accepting differences. That lead to larger assemblies where we encouraged students to embrace their own differences and to notice when someone could use a friend. Peter showed students how to have a healthy sense of humor and that finding something you're passionate about gives you a purpose. For Peter, that's playing guitar.

Our speaking engagements were cancelled during the pandemic, so we turned our attention to social media. Peter posted a few guitar videos that drew a lot of engagement. The popularity of those videos led to questions about his hearing aid and medical issues. We found that combining his guitar playing with raising awareness about his craniofacial syndrome attracted a supportive and engaged following. We've been mixing this content ever since. The best part of building a positive community is that the kindness is returned in messages like these:

You teach the world to see ability and not disability.

I haven't touched a guitar in thirty years, but you've inspired me to start playing again.

Last year was tough and watching you rock helped bring me out of a very hard time.

You're one of my favorite follows. You inspire me to do better for myself.

Knowing that our content helps others is what encourages me to continue this work. There will still be challenges and opportunities, but I'm no longer frozen with fear. I plan to make the most of whatever life presents. I hope Peter's story inspires you to do the same.

Your life is a gift; choose to rock it.
Dede Dankelson

Jacob, Dede, Darin, and Peter Dankelson
November 2021

Introduction

This is a story about choices, both the ones you make and the ones that are made for you. I believe that how you perceive both has a huge impact on your life. I know that's a big leap from someone who's only been around for two decades, but I'm not your typical twenty-one-year-old.

I was born premature with more than ten birth defects, resulting in a diagnosis of Goldenhar Syndrome. I had thirty-six surgeries during my first nineteen years, and I've grown up with the social stigma of having a facial difference. Being called names like "freak" and "Freddy Kreuger" could've easily left me feeing like a victim of circumstance.

I've refused to allow those circumstances to define my life though. I've persevered through tough recoveries, armed with a positive attitude and a sense of humor. I've built resiliency by breaking through fear to make decisions that were in my best interest. I've been blessed with a supportive family and great friends.

At fifteen, I became interested in playing guitar. The first time I held one in my hands ignited a passion that continues to burn. I became obsessed with teaching myself how to play by listening to music and watching YouTube videos. My hearing loss and hand disability did not stop me from learning; instead, they made me work harder to become a better player.

Music helps me stay positive during tough times, and playing guitar is my passion. I love sharing that passion with audiences around the world. This book is about my first twenty-one years performing on some incredibly unique stages.

Peter William Dankelson
Photo Credit - Images by Marie Moore, 2020

ONE

Born to be Different

I was born at two thirty in the morning in what my Mom describes as the scariest day of her life. It was early October, and I wasn't due until mid-December. She also knew I had significant birth defects.

My parents had been married for three years, and they'd spent the last two trying to get pregnant. After a few miscarriages and months of infertility treatments, they were overjoyed to finally be expecting.

They went to a routine ultrasound about halfway through the pregnancy, excited to see pictures of me and hear my heartbeat. They left heartbroken and full of fear and uncertainty about my future.

They were told that I had birth defects with my kidney and lower jaw. My kidney was in an unusual location, and it appeared that I only had one instead of two. Doctors also noted that my lower jaw was so small that it might block my upper airway.

These two birth defects, my parents were told, could result in incompatibility with life. The specialist's exact words were, "Where there's smoke, there's fire. The baby probably has more issues, and you should consider terminating the pregnancy." No parent is ever prepared to hear such harsh, unempathetic advice.

The doctor who said these incomprehensible words had never met my parents. He knew nothing of their journey to get pregnant or their previous miscarriages. He had no idea how much they already loved me. My Dad still gets upset when telling this story.

That doctor's inability to communicate with compassion made a lasting impression on my parents. They told him they would under no circumstances terminate, and they abruptly left his office. They knew this doctor had nothing more to offer them.

My parents were scared and worried, but they were determined to handle whatever happened. After several sleepless nights and lots of tears, Mom and Dad composed themselves and began preparing for my arrival. They consulted with Mom's obstetrician and were referred elsewhere for more tests.

Mom celebrated her thirtieth birthday with an amniocentesis followed by a 3D ultrasound. An amniocentesis (amnio) is a medical procedure where a long needle is inserted into the mother's uterus to withdraw amniotic fluid for testing. The test checks for chromosomal abnormalities.

A healthy baby has forty-six chromosomes. The amnio either confirms this or reveals any variances. This does not rule out all birth defects. My test, for example, showed that I had forty-six healthy chromosomes. So, it ruled out some but not all potential birth defects. I've always been a man of mystery!

The 3D ultrasound gave everyone a closer look at me. This

was in 2000, and 3D ultrasounds were only available through research grants. Mom and Dad intended to be surprised about my gender, but they decided to find out as a reward for going through all those tests. Talk about a unique gender reveal (that wasn't a thing back then either).

The 3D ultrasound confirmed that I had kidney and lower jaw abnormalities. My jaw was very small. In medical terms that is known as micrognathia. My kidney or kidneys were not where they should be. Most people have two kidneys that are protected behind the rib cage. I had either one large kidney or two that were fused together, and it was lower in my pelvis.

After receiving the test results and consulting with specialists, Mom and Dad chose the University of Michigan for my delivery. This is a big deal because my Dad's family is from Ohio, and he grew up cheering for the Ohio State Buckeyes. U of M and Ohio State are huge rivals, kind of like Coke vs Pepsi or Apple vs Microsoft. Despite his aversion, they knew that U of M had the best facility and specialists to take care of both Mom and me.

The team at U of M closely followed Mom's pregnancy and ordered detailed ultrasounds. All the doctors advised her to stay away from Internet research. Before the pregnancy, Mom was a market research analyst in the automotive industry. There was no way she wasn't doing her own research!

Social media didn't exist in 2000. We were still in the archaic days of dial-up Internet access, which, if you're my age or younger, you probably can't even comprehend. Try, if you can, to imagine a world without Google, Instagram, or the iPhone. I can't even fathom such ancient times!

Yahoo! was the big search engine in 2000, and Mom is resourceful. She set to work searching for conditions that had kidney and micrognathia (small jaw) birth defects. Websites like the National Organization for Rare Diseases came up where you could type in symptoms and generate lists of rare diseases. Mom learned that micrognathia is an indicator for a vast number of conditions with a wide array of severities. Some of the diseases were incompatible with life, but many were not.

Mom spent sleepless nights researching and crying. She learned that kids with micrognathia often need a tracheotomy (trach) to breathe and a feeding tube to eat. She joined listserv groups with parents who had children with airway and eating issues.

Listservs were a popular way for large groups to communicate via email before Facebook and other social platforms. Mom found comfort in learning more about kids with trachs and parents were very kind in responding to her questions. Education and preparation became her antidote to fear and grief.

During her research, Mom learned that a baby's ears are formed around the same time as the jaw and kidneys. At her twenty-nine-week ultrasound, she asked the tech if he could zoom in on my ears. The tech noted there did appear to be a difference in the size of my ears with one being smaller.

Mom found the medical terms for a small or missing ear (microtia) and a narrow or missing ear canal (atresia). She added those words to her search on kidney and micrognathia. The condition Oculo-Auriculo-Vertebral Spectrum, also known as Hemifacial Microsomia and Goldenhar Syndrome, repeatedly came up in her search results. The information scared her, and she began to understand why doctors told her to avoid the Internet.

Photos of children and adults with asymmetrical skulls and missing ears and eyes made her heart sink. She prayed this was not going to be my fate in life, but she also knew it was a definite possibility. She felt a sort of intuition when reading about Oculo-Auriculo-Vertebral Spectrum (OAVS).

Mom printed out the information to share with Dad who was away on a business trip. They unfortunately never had time to discuss it because she began having contractions the same day. She was thirty weeks pregnant, and Dad was on the other side of the country.

Mom's specialists were monitoring her for a condition called polyhydramnios, which is an excess of amniotic fluid. This was most likely due to my inability to swallow in utero. The excess fluid was building up, putting Mom at risk for premature labor. She was swelling up like a balloon, and I was floating around in a giant swimming pool!

When the contractions started, Mom's doctor advised her to drive to the local hospital that was only ten minutes from our house. We live in Michigan and didn't have any family nearby, but we did have great neighbors. Unfortunately, they were all at work. She gave our dog, Divot, a goodbye hug and expected to be home in a few hours.

Mom was in denial that this was going to be the actual event. She assumed she was having those early Braxton Hicks contractions they talk about in pregnancy books. Plus, my due date was still ten weeks away.

Mom ended up spending several hours at the local hospital where she was eventually transported in an ambulance to the

University of Michigan. She called our neighbors and asked them to take care of Divot. They did that and more.

Two of her neighbors followed the ambulance to U of M and stayed with her until late into the evening. Everyone was trying to reach Dad who was on the other side of the country. Remember, this was before everyone used mobile phones. There was no such thing as text messaging then either.

Dad was on a business trip that included a round of golf at PGA West in Palm Springs. Mom talked to him before she went to the hospital to be checked. They agreed to talk later after his round was done and when she was back from the hospital. I don't know what they were thinking!

Dad had a great round and shot a seventy-seven. His score, however, was quickly forgotten when his phone showed over forty missed calls. Panic ensued! He heard the first message and immediately called the airlines. He didn't get a call through to Mom until about midnight east coast time. By then she had arrived at U of M and was told they had no rooms available. She was camping out on a bed in the recovery area with no phone access.

Dad's flight was scheduled to land around ten o'clock a.m., so their neighbors stayed with her until two in the morning. In all the craziness, Mom forgot to call my Grandma (her Mom) who lived three hours away in Indiana. I think she was too focused on being mad at Dad and in denial about being in labor.

Mom spent a sleepless night in the recovery area. It was scary, especially when her water broke at five o'clock a.m. and she was completely alone. It is a curious thing how logistics work in hospitals. As soon as Mom's water broke, a room was available. I guess the staff realized I was going to keep causing trouble.

The best part about getting the room was access to a phone. Her first call was to Grandma who immediately began the three hour drive from Indiana to Michigan. With Dad and Grandma both on their way, I decided to stop causing trouble. Now that I had everyone's attention, I wanted to keep them in suspense!

Mom went into the hospital on second of October with my due date ten weeks away. She could not leave the hospital once her water broke, but they wanted me to stay put until Halloween. My due date was December twelfth.

The first form Mom signed was consent for an epidural. I had caused enough drama, and she had no intention of a drug-free labor and delivery. With that task completed, Mom settled in for a lengthy wait.

Doctors ordered antibiotics to prevent infection and Surfactin, a drug that speeds up lung development in utero. A baby's lungs aren't considered fully developed until about thirty-six weeks gestation, and I was six weeks away from that milestone.

After a few days with no mischief from me, Grandma headed back to Indiana. Dad was on duty and sleeping in Mom's room. He was not allowed to leave, not even if the weather was perfect for golf! Divot was bunking with the neighbor's cat and having a good time, so no worries there.

Specialists at U of M began planning for my delivery, hoping it would still be several weeks away. They discussed scheduling my arrival in an operating room with a team of specialists at the ready. The team included neonatologists and airway specialists.

Neonatologists are preemie doctors. They are experienced at intubating small airways for preemies who often need to be on a ventilator. An airway specialist was considered because of my small jaw and unique facial anatomy. There was concern that I might need to be trached emergently if specialists were unsuccessful at getting the airway tube down my throat or nose. A trach or tracheotomy is a hole created in the neck to breathe through.

I think it was nice they were planning this big party for me, but I had other plans. It turns out that Mom has a higher pain tolerance than she thought because she had been in labor (or maybe denial) for several hours without knowing. Mom was hooked up to monitors, so she figured if there was real action the experts would know. Apparently not!

Mom and Dad settled in to sleep on a Friday night. Dad drifted off quickly and was soon snoring. Mom couldn't get comfortable or stay asleep. She kept waking up. The nurse finally gave her some valium to help her relax, but even that didn't work.

Concerned, the nurse decided it was time to call a doctor. This was about two o'clock on Saturday morning. While the nurse was looking for a doctor, Mom tried to wake up Dad. She almost threw the phone at him before he finally woke up. It wasn't a light, mobile phone either!

When the doctor came in to check, Mom was already 10cm dilated. That's considered advanced labor. The nurse pulled up the bed rails and threw scrubs at Dad, telling him to put them on. Mom asked about the epidural and the nurse said it was too late. Mom said, "Are you kidding me? That's the first form I signed!"

"The good news," said the nurse, "is that you can start pushing right away." Mom did not think that was good news at all. Dad still wasn't fully awake or aware of what was happening. Good thing the nurse coached him through it all.

Everything happened very quickly. I was born in less than thirty minutes without the big party of specialists that had been planned. Dad cut the umbilical cord and caught a glimpse of me before I was whisked away to the neonatal intensive-care unit (NICU).

Mom had complications after delivery that necessitated a spinal block. Yes, she had a spinal block AFTER I was delivered. Dad stayed with her since he couldn't be anywhere near me. The NICU team went into quick action to secure my airway and make sure my vitals were stable. My blood pressure was high, and it was one of the first things addressed after getting me on a ventilator. A ventilator is a machine that breathes for you. It is sometimes called "life support."

I weighed less than three pounds and even the smallest diapers were too big. The first time Mom and Dad got a good look at me, I was already attached to several machines. They could see how small my facial bones were and that I did not have a left ear. Their hearts ached with worry that I was in pain, but nurses assured them they were managing it with medication.

Mom and Dad hoped I could hear their voices telling me how much I was loved, but they had no idea if I could hear anything. I was staying warm under bright heating lights and still had the downy hair (lanugo) that's typical on a premature

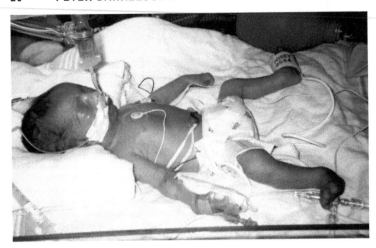

Peter William Dankelson - Born October 7, 2000
Photo Credit - Dede Dankelson, 2000

infant. My nurse asked if Mom and Dad had a name for me yet. Mom and Dad had already decided my first name would be Peter, which means "Rock." Dad is Catholic, and Peter was his confirmation name.

My middle name is William, after my maternal great grandfather who I've been blessed to grow up knowing. He's a ninety-four-year-old, chain-smoking, feisty World War II Veteran. I think they chose well, and I'm proud to be his great grandson.

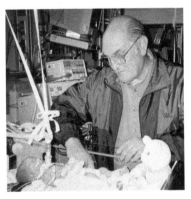

Peter in the NICU with his Great Grandpa William Winters
Photo Credit - Dede Dankelson, 2000

Mom was in the hospital for just one more night before being discharged. She and Dad had to leave the hospital with empty arms and heavy hearts. They hated leaving me in that scary open room with ten other babies.

The entire NICU at U of M had four rooms with ten beds in each. The patient's room corresponded to the level of critical care needed. Room One was the most critical with preemies as small as one pound. Room Four was the least critical. I was in Room Two.

The first night after Mom's discharge, a baby in my room became an angel. It was not the only loss that happened during my fifteen weeks there. Being in the hospital is a constant reminder of how fragile life is. You witness both heartache and miracles.

Mom and Dad saw micro-preemies fighting to live, babies in pain from drug addiction, and the miracles of modern medicine. They met other parents who deeply loved their child, and they saw babies who never felt the loving touch of a parent. They understood our journey would be a struggle, but they never lost hope.

A few days after I was born, a geneticist came to check on me. He was kind and compassionate, and Mom and Dad could tell that he was very respected by the staff. They watched as Dr. Mason Barr measured my facial features on both sides with a tiny ruler, evaluated my chart, and did a full body exam. He spoke to Mom and Dad as he examined me. He began listing my birth defects, which seemed to go on forever.

I had cleft palate (a hole in the roof of my mouth), microtia (missing left ear), atresia (missing left ear canal), hemivertebrae, c-spine defects, micrognathia (small/missing jaw), dermoid cysts in eyes, asymmetry of the face and body, a hypoplastic (small) left thumb, and a single-pelvic kidney. Mom's heart shattered with every item he listed. She wondered if she had done something during her pregnancy to cause this.

Dr. Barr said he was fairly confident he had a diagnosis, but he wanted to do a little more research before discussing it further. He also wanted to give my parents, especially Mom, time to recover from the shock of hearing the extent of my birth defects. His words were realistic but hopeful, and my parents remained grateful for his experience and kindness. Dr. Barr told them, "This is not doom and gloom, but it is a very rough road."

The contrast between that doctor's words and those of the first specialist, helped my parents understand that, like most professions, healthcare has a diverse group of personalities. They learned to work with providers who communicated with compassion and respected them as an equal member of my medical team. Doctors do not have a crystal ball. There's a reason medicine is referred to as a practice.

Dr. Barr called Dad later the same day. Mom, who was still recovering, had gone home to rest. When Dad called her with the diagnosis, she began to write down the complicated name but then stopped. She recognized the words and reached for the papers left on the printer from when she went into labor. They were the same: Oculo-Auriculo-Vertebral Spectrum, also known as Hemifacial Microsomia and Goldenhar Syndrome. Mom was already learning to trust her instincts!

The diagnosis was helpful in knowing what else to look for, like heart defects, and to begin understanding my long-term prognosis. It did not change any of the immediate interventions I needed, like the ventilator and oxygen. The greatest benefit of the diagnosis was that it narrowed Mom's research into prognosis and treatments.

She connected with online parent groups who had children with the same diagnosis. These listserv groups proved both emotionally and medically helpful. Mom learned what questions to ask, how to advocate for me, and how to become a parent different from the one she had envisioned. This online group of parents made her feel less alone. They became mentors and seeing photos of their children gave her hope for my future. This is how our journey as a family began.

We shared many firsts during those four months in NICU. We celebrated my first Halloween, Thanksgiving, Christmas, and New Year's Day in the hospital. I also had my first two surgeries during that time, and I was baptized by the hospital chaplain.

The most difficult part for Mom and Dad was not getting to hold me for several weeks. As first-time parents, they were eager to cuddle and hold me close. The machines were one obstacle, but the bigger worry was my neck and back.

To secure my airway and put me on a ventilator, doctors had to insert a breathing tube down the back of my throat into my lower lungs. This is called intubation. It is normal to take a chest x-ray after inserting the tube to make sure it's in the correct position.

When doctors reviewed my chest x-ray, they confirmed that the tube was safely in position. They also saw that the bones in my neck were not normal. There were large gaps between my neck vertebrae. Doctors grew concerned that my spinal cord was damaged.

There are seven stacked bones in your neck that make up the cervical spine, also called the c-spine. These bones protect your spinal cord and support your head. It's the part of your spinal cord that sends messages from your brain to the rest of your body. Any damage to the cervical spine can cause paralysis or the inability to move parts of your body.

The NICU doctors requested evaluations by neurosurgery and orthopedics. After reviewing my x-rays, Dr. Robert Hensinger, Chief of Orthopedics, put me on c-spine precautions. This meant that my neck was not to be moved and that no one could hold me. That was the terrifying news my parents received as Dad wheeled Mom into the NICU on their first day as parents.

After a long week of pinching me for a reaction, I finally showed movement. Dr. Hensinger, however, couldn't say with certainty that my vertebrae would support my head and protect my spinal cord. I was still less than three pounds, and it was impossible to tell how strong my bones were. He ordered the Orthopedic Team to design a body brace to protect my neck from movement.

This brace was a one-of-a-kind creation, unique as me, that was probably written about in medical texts. Mom and Dad were grateful for the safety precautions, but they also hated it. That brace remained a barrier between me and the comfort of their loving arms for over a month. They were emotionally torn between a deep desire to hold me and an overwhelming fear of hurting me.

Amidst the uncertainty of my neck issues was my airway.

Doctors worried that if my breathing tube came out, they would not be able to safely get it back in, especially without moving my neck. I was a difficult intubation, even without the c-spine restrictions.

My jaw was so small that my tongue could not lay down in my mouth. It fell backward and blocked my upper airway. A trach bypasses your mouth and nose enabling you to breathe through a hole in your neck. My parents agreed that a tracheostomy was the safest option to ensure I always had an airway. They signed their first of many surgery consents when I was just three days old.

The surgery went well, and Mom and Dad rested easier knowing I had a secure airway. The vent was attached to my trach tube, so I no longer had the breathing tube down my throat.

This allowed the nurses to put me on Mom's lap while remaining in the brace and on the ventilator. It wasn't a snuggling hold, but it was the best that could be done under the circumstances. This

Darin and Dede with Peter in his brace
Photo Credit - Sharon Brockhaus, 2000

went on for several weeks as everyone waited for me to grow. As I started getting more active, a safety belt was added to keep me from scooching out of it!

With empty arms, Mom and Dad turned their focus to my hearing. I was not responsive to noise, but I had also been very sedated. After about a month of wondering, they were told my internal ear structure looked intact.

The NICU team ordered a CAT scan and MRI of my head and neck. In reviewing these images, the Ear, Nose, and Throat Team (ENT) could see that my middle ears on both sides appeared normal. The middle ear is what transmits vibrations to create sound. My right ear had a few structural abnormalities, but they believed my hearing on that side was good. Having a normal middle ear on my left side, where the outer ear and canal was missing, was great news. It meant that I could eventually use a bone-conduction hearing aid.

Mom and Dad acted on this bit of good news. They recorded themselves reading bedtime stories and brought a CD player to the hospital. For anyone under twenty, you might need to Google, "What is a CD player?" And, if you're wondering, iPods and streaming weren't around yet either. The NICU nurses would put the headset on my right side and play the CDs when Mom and Dad were not with me.

This became a fun and positive distraction for Mom and Dad. My grandparents, aunts, uncles, cousins, and more recorded themselves reading books. I also received several CDs from a music therapist. I had quite a playlist going and was totally rocking out in the NICU! It's possible that my love for books and music started then.

It comforted Mom to know I heard loving voices and music when she could not be there to whisper in my ear. She spent hours a day caressing the spot in between my eyebrows. It was one of the few places I did not have a needle or piece of equipment attached.

I had my first hearing test when I was a month old. It was

called a brainstem auditory evoked response (BAER), and it was done by using electrodes that measure auditory nerve activity. The audiologist told Mom that I had almost normal hearing in my right ear, confirming what ENT told them a few weeks earlier.

Testing my left side was trickier because I had no canal to insert the electrode. The audiologist tried using a bone conduction device instead. Unfortunately, the NICU room was too noisy. Apparently, my roommates liked to party! It was recommended that we try a second test in about a month and hope for a quieter day.

Mom and Dad remained anxious to hold me and asked often about when the next set of x-rays would be ordered. I finally had a scan after over a month of waiting. It looked promising and Mom and Dad had an intense meeting with Dr. Hensinger. He showed them my x-rays, so they could clearly see that the bones in my neck were not spaced equally apart. He said they could hold me without the brace, but they had to be careful with my neck. He was still worried that neck movement too far forward or backward would damage my spinal cord.

Mom was desperate to hold me but had a lot of anxiety that she would cause permanent damage. Dad was more excited than afraid. He knew Dr. Hensinger wouldn't let him hold me if it was too risky. He believed I was going to be fine. Those emotions of fear and joy are etched in my parents' memories when they recall their time in the NICU.

After thirty-nine anxious days, they both took a turn holding me without the brace. I don't remember, but I'm pretty sure it felt incredible to be free of that body brace. Mom was

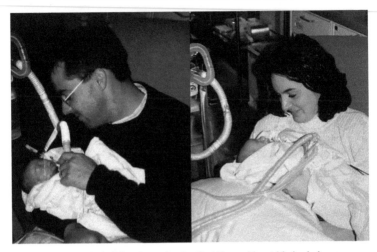

Darin & Dede holding Peter for the first time without his body brace
Photo Credit - Holden NICU Staff - November 15, 2000

extra cautious as the nurses placed me in her arms. Dad was too, of course, but he was less worried. It's a guy thing!

Mom gradually became more confident that she wasn't going to hurt me. Days in the NICU following my partial break from the brace included a lot of snuggle time. My grandparents were excited to finally hold me, and I loved every second of it!

With few exceptions, my parents were both with me every day. Mom arrived in the mornings and spent the day helping nurses take care of me. She spoke with specialists as they made rounds, and she learned everything she could about my care.

Dad arrived after work to take the evening shift. He and Mom often had dinner at the hospital and spent time together with me before Mom headed home. Dad and I bonded over bath time and bedtime trach care. He almost always tucked me in for the night.

Mom was mentally exhausted after spending a day in the NICU, and it was hard to repeatedly update family and friends over long phone conversations. She knew everyone was worried about me though, and she appreciated their concern.

Mom discovered that writing in my voice was good therapy for her. She began sending daily journal updates in an email with the subject as "Pete's Diary." Mom would come home from the hospital and write about what happened that day—who visited, gifts I received, doctors that came to see me, medical tests and results, what was next, and so on.

Pete's Diary became a viral blog before social media existed. It was forwarded to hundreds of people who read it every morning with their coffee. Remember, this was in the days of dial-up Internet access. Smart phones and broadband hadn't been invented yet. People still printed emails to read on paper!

Darin, Dede, and Peter in the NICU
Photo Credit - Sharon Brockhaus, 2000

My parents were comforted by the kind comments and well wishes. People throughout the country were following my journey, and we felt the healing power of their prayers and love. My family was grateful for the outpouring of support. One of the most powerful lessons we learned is that the darkest of times often reveals the best parts of humanity.

This community of support formed a foundation of resiliency around our family. This strength was needed as my parents navigated insurance coverage, accepted the full responsibility of my daily medical care, and learned how to advocate on my behalf.

As Fall turned into Winter, I grew stronger but was unable to fully wean off the ventilator. The hospital agreed to let me go home with a ventilator, but only if we could secure several hours of daily nursing care. That's when Mom and Dad learned that private insurance doesn't cover private-duty nursing. The hospital helped Mom petition to our private insurance and to the state for assistance. They also referred her to an attorney. Our private insurance denied everything, and the state offered no assistance without a Medicaid Waiver.

Mom could write another book about all of this, but it wouldn't be a very fun read. During the weeks of fighting with the insurance company, I grew strong enough to breathe on my own without the ventilator. That meant the hospital would allow me to go home without the required nursing hours.

Mom and Dad had to prove they could care for both me and my equipment before I could be discharged. The hospital set us up on a weekend field trip at a hotel that was attached to the building. This was our first time being alone together as a family.

We took stroller rides around the hospital, and I watched football with Dad. He wanted to make sure I wasn't becoming a Wolverine. The NICU nurses, knowing he was an Ohio State fan, liked to put Michigan booties on me when he wasn't looking!

Mom took lots of photos, which had to get developed on

real paper back then. They experienced their first of many sleepless nights and encountered one unplanned incident when I pulled the NG tube out of my nose.

An NG or nasogastric tube is inserted through the nose, down the throat, and into the stomach. It's needed if you are unable to chew or swallow food. I still couldn't take a bottle and remained completely reliant on the NG tube for nutrition.

Therapists worked with me to take a special Haberman bottle for cleft babies. My small jaw, cleft palate, and breathing issues proved too much though. Nurses taught Mom and Dad how to insert the tube and check to make sure it was correctly positioned in my stomach. Thank goodness Dad was confident and able to get it back in place because Mom was very uncomfortable with it.

Knowing I would need a longer-term solution for eating, Mom and Dad had already agreed to have a gastrostomy tube placed before I went home. The surgery was scheduled for the Monday after our weekend hotel stay. A gastrostomy or g-tube is inserted directly into your stomach and looks like a button on an inflatable raft. Liquid nutrition is pushed directly into the tube using syringes or a pump.

The NICU staff congratulated Mom and Dad on surviving the weekend with me and my gear. They all agreed it was time to put discharge plans in motion. My g-tube surgery went well, and Mom and Dad were trained in how to use the feeding pump and syringes. Home medical equipment was ordered, follow-up clinics were scheduled, our house was inspected, and Mom and Dad completed all the necessary training. It was overwhelming, especially for Mom.

Our closest family was three hours away, and Dad was often gone overnight for work. Mom, therefore, was my 24/7 caregiver. She wanted to bring me home, but she would miss the support and encouragement of the NICU nurses. She nervously joked that Divot would be her helper at home.

Mom was also worried that I was becoming more attached to the nurses than to her. They spoiled me and took me on field trips around the unit at night. It was great fun for me, but not the most soothing setting.

The NICU was noisy with bright lights, and there was no privacy. Some days my room would be converted into an operating room and closed off for hours. Mom and Dad did not like this being my daily environment. They felt I was becoming institutionalized.

I was born on October 7th and went home on January 16th. After one hundred and two days, I finally saw the world outside the hospital, took my first car ride, and made my first friend.

Divot had been smelling hospital scents for months but meeting me was the first time he connected the smell with a small human. He was fascinated, and we quickly became partners in mischief. Divot was my first best friend.

Divot with Darin and Peter during a tube-feeding
Photo Credit - Dede Dankelson - January 16, 2001

TWO

Living a Medically-Complex Life

Life without the NICU support was more challenging than my parents anticipated. I slept in their bedroom where they were up all night turning off monitor alarms, suctioning my trach, or cleaning up the bed after formula leaked from my feeding tube. Days were consumed with cleaning the equipment, early intervention therapy and day-long clinic appointments. My parents were exhausted.

The trach made me susceptible to the smallest of germs, and a small sniffle would put me back in the hospital. I required oxygen at night and was rushed to the ER in respiratory distress on multiple occasions. Dad was travelling often for work, so Mom was typically the one hanging out in the ER with me.

At my first craniofacial clinic, we were told I needed a cranial molding helmet to reshape my skull. The back of my head was flat and misshapen both from Goldenhar Syndrome and laying in the NICU brace for so many weeks.

Babies wearing cranial helmets aren't an unusual sight anymore, but they were in 2001. Mom struggled emotionally with adding it to my daily care. It was some-thing else that drew un-wanted attention.

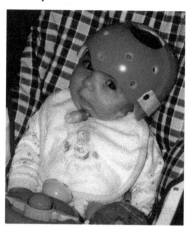

Peter wearing his cranial helmet
Photo Credit - Dede Dankelson, 2001

She felt like people were either staring at her with pity or passing judgement that she did something wrong when she was pregnant. She still had a bad case of "Mommy Guilt."

Getting the helmet also involved adding a new specialist to our growing list of appointments. I had multiple checkups and two helmets made during the nine months of wearing one. It was worth it though, because I have a beautifully shaped head now!

My third surgery was shortly after I turned a year old. I had a large cyst growing rapidly in my left lower eyelid. Dermoid cysts are non-cancerous growths that are common with Gold-enhar Syndrome, and there are different types. I had cysts in both eyes. The one in my right eye was flat and on the white part of my eye. It did not obstruct my vision, so there was no reason to remove it. The left cyst bulged out of my lower eye-lid and grew rapidly. It was creating muscle weakness and vi-sion problems.

Dr. Steven Archer, my ophthalmologist at University of Michigan's Kellogg Eye Center, had been monitoring both cysts since birth. When I was approaching twelve months old, he told Mom it was time to "debulk" the left one. The surgery was anticipated to take about an hour, but the cyst was much larger than Dr. Archer realized. It wrapped over two hundred and seventy degrees around my eye and was entwined with the eye muscles.

The surgery was outpatient, so I was home with a bandaged eye the same day. For about a week, I looked like a scrappy baby who lost a fight. When we went for my first post-op appointment, Mom learned that the cyst had weakened my left eye. Dr. Archer told her to patch my right eye for several hours every day.

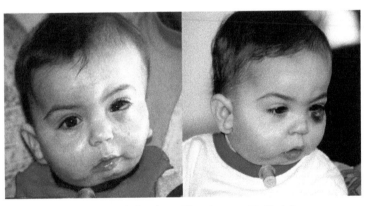

Peter before and after dermoid cyst removal in his left eye
Photo Credit - Dede Dankelson, 2001

Patching the right eye forced me to exercise the left one. It wasn't an easy task keeping an eye patch on an active one year old, but it didn't seem to hold me back.

Physical therapy worked with me two to three times a week

to build strength and correct torticollis, which is a shortened muscle on one side of the neck. I tilted my head to the right because the neck muscles on my left side were tight and weak, one of the many gifts I received from having Goldenhar Syndrome.

I needed a therapist to stretch those neck muscles, so I could hold my head straight. I also needed to get stronger. I never developed the upper body strength to crawl on my hands and knees, but I did do the "army crawl" on my belly.

My lower body was weak from my refusal to put weight on my legs. Whenever someone stood me on their lap, I would lift my feet. Mom and Dad believed my resistance to standing was from all the labs I needed in the NICU. Nurses poked my toe multiple times a week to check blood-gas levels.

Getting a doorway swing encouraged me to start jumping. Once I realized how fun it was, I was bouncing all over the place. Gaining overall strength enabled me to start cruising the furniture until I eventually took my first steps at sixteen months.

My graduation from physical therapy was met more with relief than celebration. Mom and Dad were grateful I was walking and happy to have one less therapist to work with. Every milestone I achieved eased their anxiety.

After six to nine months of patching, Mom was given the good news that I no longer needed to patch my right eye. The good news was met with bad. I needed another eye surgery to open a blocked tear duct. When a tear duct is blocked, the eye can't drain properly. This causes irritation and is a risk for infection.

I went through a series of eye surgeries to open the tear

duct. Dr. Archer probed the tear duct first to see if it would stay open. It didn't, so I had a subsequent surgery where he inserted a tube to keep the duct open. This resulted in a very memorable night one weekend.

Mom and Dad had become friends with two other couples in our neighborhood. They were all about the same age and starting families. We often got together on Friday or Saturday nights for pizza and fun. One of those nights, just after I had the tube put in my eye, it popped out.

You can imagine the surprise on everyone's face when they saw a long tube hanging out of my eyeball! It was still attached somewhere inside my eye but had come loose. Mom had been warned this might happen, but she was still freaked out.

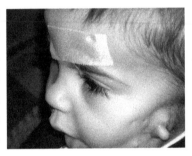

Peter with a loose tube in his eye
Photo Credit - Dede Dankelson, 2003

They ended up taping the tube to my forehead and giving the doctor a call. He said they could cut the tube and gently pull it out. This was a bit unsettling, and Mom was worried I would move my head suddenly when the scissors were close. One of my home nurses was scheduled to come the night after this happened, so they waited for her to be there and help.

Dr. Archer checked me out the following week and decided to wait and see if the tear duct would remain open. Thankfully, it did, and no further eye surgeries were necessary. Thank goodness for that news because Mom desperately needed something to go well. This was an exhausting and precarious time for both my health and her sanity.

I was constantly in respiratory distress, and Mom began having panic attacks when left alone with me. She was also working through the loss of her younger brother who unexpectedly died just after my first birthday.

When the person holding everything together begins to crack, life for everyone becomes unstable. Dad realized this and helped Mom find the support she needed to work through the grief and depression. It gave Mom the strength to keep fighting for home nursing help.

The lawyer Mom spoke with when I was still in the NICU had told her about the Children's Medicaid Waiver. This program waived income and approved cases based on the child and family's need. Every state has one of these programs and manages it differently. In Michigan, there were a maximum of one hundred spots, and they were always full.

For two years, Mom wrote letters and made phone calls to a case worker pleading our case for the Medicaid Waiver. The program is based on a scoring system that includes both medical and family need. I exceeded all the medical points, but we did not score high enough as a family.

To increase our score, my parents needed to have another child, divorce, and/or have documented mental health needs. The attorney said our only hope of receiving the waiver was to write a letter to the state requesting that I be placed in foster care. Mom needed to put in writing that she could no longer take care of me.

She knew this for two years and refused to write the letter. After her breakdown, Mom was done fighting. She wrote the letter and sent it knowing we would never follow through with the threat.

I was immediately moved from fortieth on the waiting list to third. We were approved for seventy-two hours of nursing care per week, enough to have someone monitor me on eight hour shifts overnight. After two years, I was finally moved out of Mom and Dad's bedroom and into my own place!

While the nursing help was a relief, it is not ideal to have strangers in your house at night. As with anything funded by the government, the price for help was our privacy.

State workers came into our house constantly questioning our need for the waiver and threatening to take it away. On several occasions, Mom was verbally attacked by case workers who accused her of being a bad parent and disorganized. Dad intervened at one point and said that one particular case worker was no longer welcome in our home.

We eventually found nurses we could trust, but that was after going through several that were either sleeping on the job or unreliable. The nursing care gave Mom the sleep and security she needed to recover. This was critical because I endured fifteen more surgeries between the ages of two and four.

Five of the surgeries were what we call, "big ones". The first of those was my cleft palate repair where surgeons closed the hole in the roof of my mouth. This was done by Dr. Arlene Rozzelle at Children's Hospital of Michigan, just before my second birthday.

The surgery went well, and I was transferred to the pediatric intensive care unit (PICU) for recovery. Swelling peaks about forty-eight hours post-op, and Dr. Rozzelle wanted me under close observation during that time.

Mom and Dad couldn't sleep in the PICU overnight, so Dad stayed in the waiting room to be on call. Grandma, who drove in from Indiana, and Mom headed back to our house. We lived about an hour from the hospital, so it wasn't an easy commute.

They drove back in the morning to relieve Dad. The plan was for me to stay in the PICU a couple nights. By twenty-four hours post-op, however, I was up and dancing in the hallway.

The PICU staff contacted Dr. Rozzelle about either a discharge or moving me out of intensive care. As Dad was headed back for his night shift, Mom called to tell him we were packing up to go home. We were all happy to finish my recovery from the couch. Divot was especially happy to have us back.

Having the home nursing care at night enabled all three of us to rest and recover. This was important because Mom and Dad had big decisions to make regarding my medical plans. They needed to research and find surgeons with the expertise and experience to improve my ability to breathe, eat, and speak normally.

Mom and Dad had opinions from four surgeons about how and when to reconstruct my jaw, and they were all different. Some felt I should wait a few more years before having the surgeries, while others advised it best to have them now. Some would require my mouth to be wired shut, while others did not. Some were out of state and would require extra work to be approved by our insurance. It was all very time consuming and confusing.

It took several months of consultations, phone calls, and paperwork before a decision was made. Mom and Dad chose an out of state surgeon who was often recommended in Mom's parent groups. Dr. Jeffrey Marsh operated at St. Louis Children's Hospital.

For my first surgery, he would harvest a rib and graft it to my left mandible (lower jaw) where I was missing bone. The subsequent surgeries would involve lengthening my jaw through a process called distraction.

We would travel to and from St. Louis for these surgeries, and I would be monitored at home by Dr. Rozzelle at Children's Hospital of Michigan. My parents felt good about this plan and having the surgeons work together. Dr. Marsh had a unique way of doing the rib graft that did not require wiring my mouth shut for several weeks.

This was a relief to Mom because I had reflux and often vomited several times a day on the tube feedings. After multiple visits and medication trials with a GI (gastrointestinal) specialist, this eventually improved. Still, it was a scary thought that I could easily aspirate and choke to death with my mouth wired shut.

The rib graft surgery went well, and Mom learned that she couldn't plan for everything. As they waited, my parents received a phone call from the operating room. They were expecting to receive a few updates on how things were going, but they weren't planning to be asked about moving my earlobe.

The surgery was on my left side where I was missing my entire outer ear. I did have a small earlobe on that side, but it was lower than where it should've been. Dr. Marsh wanted to know if he should move my left earlobe to align it with my right side.

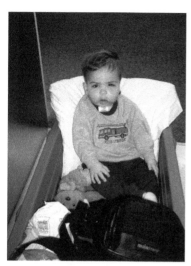

Peter at St. Louis Children's Hospital
Photo Credit - Dede Dankelson, 2003

Mom hadn't done much research about this, but she knew that scar tissue might encumber future reconstruction of an outer ear. So, it was not an easy decision. In the end, Mom and Dad agreed to have the earlobe moved. This was ultimately a good decision, but it gave Mom a lot of stress. The skin turned completely black, and she worried for weeks that I would lose it.

After a few nights in St. Louis, I was discharged and headed home to Divot. The remainder of my recovery went well, and Dr. Rozzelle's craniofacial team in Detroit did a great job monitoring my healing and communicating with Dr. Marsh in St. Louis. After about nine months, the rib bone was healthy enough to schedule the distraction.

Mom says the jaw distraction was the worst of my surgeries during this time. The initial surgery in St. Louis went well. Dr. Marsh placed the device inside my jaw where it couldn't be seen, but I did have two pins that protruded from my small chin. These had to be accessible so that someone could turn them three times a day for two weeks.

Turning each pin lengthened the internal device, prompting my body to fill in the gap by growing new bone. Every turn created about a one-millimeter gap. The goal was to get twelve to fourteen millimeters of new bone growth. We hoped that lengthening my jaw by that much would enable my tongue to lay flat inside my mouth. This would prevent my tongue from falling back and blocking my upper airway. If we could achieve that, I might be able to get rid of the trach.

I screamed every time Mom and Dad took a screwdriver to the pins and turned them. One of them would hold my head still while the other turned the pins. Taking a screwdriver to your child's face is something no parent should endure. It was excruciating for them both.

I was monitored by Dr. Rozzelle at Children's Hospital of Michigan in Detroit during this process. She noticed that my skin was looking red and inflamed. The pins were turning at odd angles and coming in close contact with my trach. Secretions from the trach were causing an infection to develop. Dr. Rozzelle had me immediately admitted to start I.V. antibiotics.

After more than three unsuccessful attempts to start the I.V., Mom called it off. She couldn't stand the trauma of watching me scream as I was held down under bright lights in the treatment room. She insisted they find another way. After some debate, I was taken to pre-op where I was sedated to successfully get the I.V. started.

I spent a week at Children's Hospital of Michigan in Detroit and was discharged with a PICC line to continue the antibiotics at home. A PICC (peripherally inserted central catheter) is essentially a long-term I.V. Mom and Dad were trained on how to care for it. They were once again grateful for my home-care nurses who were a tremendous help during this time.

The PICC line was inserted by an angioplasty surgeon

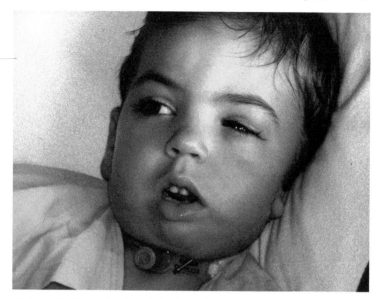

Peter at Children's Hospital of Michigan with an infection from jaw distraction
Photo Credit - Dede Dankelson 2003

while I was under anesthesia. She told Mom and Dad that she nearly gave up after several attempts, but a nurse encouraged her to keep trying. I had very challenging veins!

Divot loved all the new hospital smells when I returned home, and we had a great time scaring Mommy. She had my arm under secure wraps so nothing would pull on that critical PICC line. After a few weeks of this fun, I went back to the operating room where both the PICC line and external pins were removed. The internal device would remain for several months.

With the complications, it was easy to forget why we were doing all this—to enlarge my upper airway. Mom had taken a profile photo before the surgery, so they could compare. It

Peter before and after jaw distraction
Photo Credit - Dede Dankelson, 2003

was noticeably different, and they were hopeful my new jaw might be large enough to get the trach removed.

Following several months of healing, I had another surgery to remove the internal device. We were finally at the end of the jaw reconstruction process. Would it enable me to breathe through my mouth and nose? We'd have to consult with Dr. Walter Belenky, my ENT at Children's Hospital of Michigan, to find out.

The first step in this process was capping my trach a few hours every day. This went on for several months, and I did fine breathing through my mouth and nose. The next test was a sleep study to see if I could breathe safely at night. Laying down was the hardest position for me to breathe because that is when my tongue would fall back and block my airway.

My sleep study results were disappointing. Mom and Dad were crushed over this news. Dr. Belenky scheduled a bronchoscopy to get an inside look at my upper airway. A bronchoscopy is done in the operating room under sedation. A small camera secured to the end of a tube is put down your throat or nose.

Even with the jaw reconstruction, my upper airway was extremely narrow. It was at such a sharp angle that surgeons couldn't get the camera past my nose or throat into my lungs. The only way they could look at the furthest part of my upper airway was to put the camera through my trach hole and flip it around to see upward. My jaw structure was improved, but other parts of my anatomy were still limiting my ability to breathe normally.

There was nothing more to do but wait and try again in six to nine months. It was time to accept the trach would be a longer part of my life. These surgeries happened from the ages of two to four. I don't remember them, but I can tell you that my body certainly does. Enduring so much physical and emotional trauma, even when you are too young to remember it, stays with you. I have read the body remembers what the mind forgets, and I believe that to be true.

As a toddler, I would start crying as soon as our car merged onto the highway toward the hospital. I called the operating room, "The White Room" and would plead not to be taken back there. My parents, especially Mom, who took me to every appointment, were also impacted by this trauma. Imagine hearing your child scream, "Please, Mommy, I'll do anything. Please don't let them hurt me."

My medical trauma was not just from the surgeries. I had frequent follow up clinics to check my kidney, back and neck, stomach, heart, lungs, and hearing. I had so many specialists that Mom kept them listed in a spreadsheet. All these appointments involved procedures like blood draws, sleep studies, x-rays, CT scans, MRIs, and hearing tests that added to my anxiety. I eventually understood which ones involved needles and which ones just seemed scary, but it all took a toll.

I had so much anxiety walking into a dark radiology lab that I would throw up just from being in the room. Any time I heard the word "labs," my body would immediately go into a state of panic. Between I.V.s for surgeries and frequent blood draws, I developed a huge phobia of needles. I would fight and scream so much that technicians would eventually wrap me up in blankets and hold me down to get the job done. Sometimes it took three to four people to hold me still. It was excruciating for both me and Mom.

Sleep studies do not involve needles, but they are uncomfortable and scary to a toddler. Dad always took me to the sleep studies and had to hold me down while technicians stuck sensors on my head and body. Having strangers constantly come at you makes you fearful of everything that is unfamiliar. I became resistant about trying anything new or different, even if it was something intended to be fun, like going

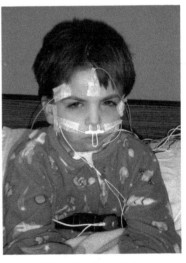

Peter at a sleep study
Photo Credit - Dede Dankelson, 2004

to a new playground. My body was always on alert.

This became more apparent as we began venturing out into the world. We were primarily homebound my first three years. Mom wouldn't even take me into a store for fear I would catch a cold and end up back in the hospital. It was also necessary to self-isolate for weeks before each surgery to make sure I didn't get sick.

As we began doing normal activities like going to the zoo, Mom was the one to feel anxious. She hated how kids would chase me around the playground trying to touch my trach or little ear, and she wasn't used to navigating these social situations.

Mom also had a lot of self-inflicted guilt about others judging her. She still felt responsible for my birth defects, and it made her even more self-conscious around other parents. She knew, though, that I would one day look to her and Dad as an example for how to react to the staring.

Mom chose to interact directly with the kids. If they were wearing a character shirt, she would say, "Peter likes Blue's Clues too. Who is your favorite character?" Sometimes this would help the situation and other times the kids would run away. Sometimes their parents brought them back, but often parents moved elsewhere or awkwardly pretended to ignore the situation.

Mom would return home frustrated, thinking that there had to be more she could do to build a supportive community around me. She wanted to educate others about my condition and to let people know that we were comfortable talking about it.

Mom discussed this with Dad, and they came up with the idea of hosting a golf tournament in our neighborhood. Dad is a golfer, and we lived in a golf course community. Mom also wanted this to be about more than just me. She knew of a few charities that supported families affected by craniofacial differences. One stood out to her, and she dedicated the tournament to Children's Craniofacial Association or CCA Kids.

She liked how CCA connected families through their annual retreats. They host a four-day event in a different part of the country every year where families affected by facial differences come together. The weekend provides instant bonding, friendship, and one hundred percent fun. No needles or white coats allowed!

Because of my fragile health and busy surgery schedule, we had not attended a CCA retreat. Mom wanted to get more involved though, and she thought the golf tournament was a great way to start.

We hosted our first *Pete's Scramble for CCA* in 2003. It was a small but fun gathering of family and friends. The tournament achieved everything Mom hoped for in raising awareness within our community, and it became an annual event for five consecutive years.

Educating our neighborhood made home a relaxing place for all of us. Kids in our neighborhood were used to my differences, and Mom never felt anxious with me playing outside. We were included at parties and gatherings just like everyone else.

The playground remained a challenge, but Mom eventually realized that I was her best judge of character. She noticed that I had a sense of who was genuinely concerned about me and who had bad intentions. So, she stopped intervening and began to follow my lead.

Accepting she could never control how others reacted to my differences was empowering. Mom's worry over what might happen when we went somewhere gradually stopped. She found herself not even thinking about my differences until someone else pointed them out. When people stared, she would stare back and smile. This was usually enough to nudge someone to stop staring or encourage them to start a conversation.

Mom knew I was getting old enough to notice the staring, and she wanted to be a good example of how to deal with it. One thing she learned was that my differences left a memorable impression, and we always had a choice in how we reacted. If possible, Mom wanted that impression to be positive. She believed leaving a good impression taught others that differences are nothing to fear or feel insecure about.

This is the approach we practiced as I moved into the preschool years. I was in early intervention therapy and classes off and on between my surgeries, but I had yet to be left at a school without Mom nearby. She was never comfortable leaving me alone with anyone other than Dad or a trained nurse, which is one of the reasons we wanted the trach removed. Mom knew it was going to require extra supervision at school. With that situation indefinitely on hold, Mom turned her focus toward teaching me to eat. That, she knew, would also be an issue when I attended longer days at school.

I hated anything to do with food and could not even sit in front of a plate without gagging. Speech, occupational, and physical therapy were a regular part of my life from birth to five. It was not unusual for me to have four to eight hours of therapy weekly, and a lot of it was focused on trying to help me chew, swallow, and overcome the fear of textures and tastes.

Mom and I did a lot of finger painting with pudding and shaving cream, pulling objects out of dry rice and popcorn kernels, building sandcastles, and making things with Play-Doh. We also did brushing therapy and oral stimulation exercises with all kinds of crazy therapy tools. Some of it helped with my sensory issues, but none of it motivated me to eat.

I consumed most of my calories overnight through a feeding pump, so I wasn't hungry during the day. Did you know that hunger is learned if you don't develop it in your first three months of life? Most of us assume it is an instinct we are born with. That's true, but only in the first few months. Well-meaning people would often tell Mom, "he'll eat when he's hungry." They did not understand that I had no idea how to eat or what hungry even meant.

Mom was frustrated with lack of progress and needed a break. She was also pregnant and knew she could not keep up with the therapy once my brother arrived. I have to say, it's a good thing she recognized that before he was born because he was seriously high maintenance. He cried nonstop those first few months they brought him home. Divot and I often wore earmuffs!

I was four and done with my first round of major surgeries the summer before Jacob was born. While we waited to learn if I could breathe without the trach, Mom turned her full attention on my eating issues.

Mom was on a few email groups with other parents who had children with trachs, feeding tubes, and Goldenhar Syndrome. These parents were a wealth of information. Mom had a lot of support and tips about feeding therapy and blending foods to transition from the tube. She went to work pureeing foods from recipes those parents shared.

Three times a day Mom would struggle to sit me down at the table and consume pureed foods. I fought it every step of the way. Mom tried everything from time outs to reward charts. She even had Santa Claus call me in July to remind me he was watching all year! I was having none of it. We were both frustrated and exhausted, especially pregnant Mom.

Since I drank water through a straw, Mom changed tactics and goals. I was four, and she was getting more anxious about navigating school with a trach and feeding tube. She wanted me to sit with my peers at lunch and not be in an office getting a tube feeding.

Mom focused on getting me comfortable drinking a can of PediaSure. This, she reasoned, would enable me to stay in the lunchroom at school instead of going to a separate office for a tube feeding. That would be one less piece of equipment to deal with.

This was a good compromise. I built up a tolerance for drinking through the straw and was able to consume the calories quickly enough to make it through a school day. Mom considered it a win, and I earned a nice break. I mean, I seriously hated food—even ice cream!

I eventually consumed all my daily nutrition by mouth instead of through the tube. It was still all liquid, but I wasn't relying on the equipment anymore. Dad was still persistent at making me try foods during mealtimes, but Mom was done. She hoped that being in school would motivate me to want to eat like the other kids. Spoiler alert... it didn't.

Mom looks back on that time as the "trach-plugging-pregnancy-food-fight" summer. There was a sense of relief that my jaw surgeries were done, and I was finally doing "normal" things like potty training. Everyone but me was excited about the arrival of my baby brother who was due in November. I kept telling my parents we should call him Oscar and have him live in a trash can!

Throughout that summer, ENT gradually downsized and plugged my trach. My breathing remained strong, and I had more sleep studies that reflected better results. We finally got the go ahead to schedule an overnight stay in the hospital. This was to remove the trach tube and observe me without it for twenty-four hours. It's called decannulation.

Mom told me we were having a "trach party" at the hospital, but I was suspicious. What kind of party involves white coats?!? Not one I'm interested in attending.

Mom, who was eight months pregnant at the time, got me settled into a room and tried to make it fun. A nurse came in and removed my trach, which was both exciting and scary. I was four years old and never knew life without the trach. To have it suddenly gone was strange.

Mom breathed a sigh of relief when the nurse wrote his name on the white board in my room. It said, "Justin." She took that as a good sign because that was my uncle's name. I don't remember Uncle Justin because he passed away when I was only one, but I know he's always looking out for me.

Dad came after work to relieve Mom and her big belly. Us guys had a good night and left the next morning with no trach. That's when the real party started!

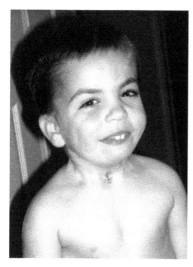

Peter with the trach tube removed
Photo Credit - Dede Dankelson, 2004

I had two blissful, trach-free weeks before "*Oscar*" showed up. He unfortunately did not live in a trash can, and everyone called him Jacob instead of Oscar. Talk about a party crasher!

Baby Jacob would not stop crying, and he totally took all the attention away from me. I still don't know what all the fuss was about. Divot didn't either. He and I mostly just tried to escape the noise.

I started early-intervention preschool a few months before Jacob arrived. I still had the trach then, and Mom was not comfortable having me there without a nurse in the building. She sat outside the preschool room and volunteered to help the teachers.

Mom knew it was a short-term solution with Jacob on the way, so the school eventually agreed to train a one-to-one aid who would be with me all the time. That was also a short-term necessity since the trach was gone by October.

Once the trach was out, Mom even let me ride the bus. I think having a newborn may have influenced her decision. I loved riding the bus and experiencing my first little bit of independence.

The other big change that happened around this time is the loss of our home nursing care. With the trach out, I no longer needed monitoring at night. Mom had been fighting to keep it for the last two years. State workers were in and out of our house almost weekly insulting, questioning, and threatening to take it away. Once the trach was out, Mom was more than happy to give it up.

Although we had some great nurses, my parents never enjoyed having people work in their house at night. Having the nursing care gone also reduced Mom's stress level with fighting for it all the time. It was a win for all of us!

Once Jacob stopped crying 24/7, I decided he was tolerable. Divot especially warmed up to him once he started eating Cheerios and solid foods. He was messy and left a smorgasbord on the floor! The two of us agreed to let him stay, as he became more interactive.

Mom says that Jacob's birth healed parts of her heart that were torn from when I was born. She says her three

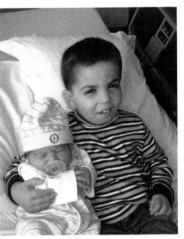

Peter and Jacob Dankelson
Photo Credit - Dede Dankelson, 2004

best days are her wedding, the day she learned she was pregnant with me, and the day Jacob was born. I like to remind her she was on a lot of "happy" drugs when Jacob was delivered via c-section. That's all I'm saying!

With Mom in a happier state of mind and major surgeries over for the near-term, we gratefully settled into a more typical family life. Mom and Dad loved seeing Jacob develop through all the baby stages of rolling over, first solids, and crawling. I never reached some of those milestones and the ones I did hit were often celebrated with a sense of relief more than joy.

Mom and Dad were more comfortable travelling, so we attended our first CCA Family Retreat when Jacob was six months old. The 2005 retreat was held in Nashville, Tennessee, and what I noticed right away was there were no white coats in sight!

For the first time I saw kids my age with feeding tubes and little ears. I floated around in the hotel pool with other kids who had trachs, and we had a big dance party. It was three days that established lifelong friendships and an even bigger desire to support this charity.

Peter with friends at the CCA Retreat
Photo Credit - Dede Dankelson, 2005

THREE

Realizing I was Different

Kindergarten was when I started feeling separate and noticing my facial differences. It was the first time I was in a mainstream group of peers, and I wanted to be part of all the action. Spending so much time at home and in hospitals left me a bit socially delayed. I had not experienced the interaction most kids acquire by that age. I was slightly over eager to make friends, but can you really blame me?

What I wanted more than anything was to fit in and look like everyone else. Having two ears, five-year-old me reasoned, would achieve that goal. That is what I wanted for my fifth birthday, a big ear! I asked my parents if they could take me to an ear store to buy one.

Mom and Dad were aware that ear reconstruction was an option, but they did not want to put me through unnecessary surgeries. Every surgery I had was medically necessary to help me eat, breathe, see, and hear. Having an external ear would not improve my hearing, and the reconstruction process involved multiple surgeries over several months. My parents were also not impressed with the before and after photos they saw.

Mom researched other options and learned about facial prosthetics. She found a Prosthetic Specialist in Ashburn, Virginia who made lifelike ears. His name was Robert Barron of Custom Prosthetic Designs, Inc. After phone conversations and more battles with our insurance company, we hit the road. During the drive, I repeatedly asked, "Are we at the ear store yet?"

I was not disappointed when we arrived at Mr. Barron's office. He is a talented artist who was Master of Disguise for the CIA for 25 years. His studio is full of fake body parts like eyes, noses, fingers, and ears! After retiring from the CIA, Mr. Barron chose to help kids like me instead of pursuing a career in Hollywood makeup. He also helps burn and cancer survivors restore their identity. It is truly an honor to know him.

On our first visit, Mr. Barron created a cast of my right ear. From that, he sculpted a mirror image out of clay. On our second visit, he used the clay sculpture to create a two-piece mold. He filled it with silicone, and we waited for it to cure. When the molds were separated, I could see my silicone ear. I had to sit very still while he painted it to be an exact match of my right ear. It was fascinating to watch the prosthetic come to life!

The "big ear" changed my life. It lessened the stares and whispers, and it gave me a lot of confidence growing up. I was proud wearing it to school every day, and Mom was happy my glasses weren't crooked anymore. She became an expert at applying the adhesive and lining it up to fit securely. In addi-

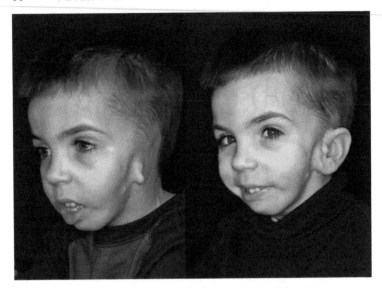

Peter before and after left prosthetic ear made by Robert Barron
Photo Credit - Custom Prosthetic Designs, Inc., 2005

tion to breakfast and brushing my teeth, we added "putting on your ear" to our morning routine.

On days that I didn't wear the prosthetic, the staring came back. One of those times was at Disney World. We were in line at the Jedi Training Academy, which was like a dream come true for me being such a huge Star Wars fan. As we waited this kid would not stop staring.

It was making Mom and I both uncomfortable, and she knew he was going to say something. When he finally said, "What happened to your ear?" Mom was ready. She said, "Oh, he was here yesterday, and Darth Vader cut it off." His eyes just about popped out of his head!

We had a good laugh over that one. Mom quickly told him that was not true and that he would survive the Jedi Training Academy with both ears still on his head. She said I was born

Peter wearing his prosthetic left ear made by Robert Barron
Photo Credit - Custom Prosthetic Designs, Inc., 2005

with only one ear, but I could still hear on my right side. He was a bit shaken, but the staring stopped!

Growing up with the prosthetic ear enabled me to blend in. What I learned though is that changing how I looked did not change who I was on the inside. I still loved Star Wars and Legos, and I still didn't like to draw or color. I was interested in the same activities and social groups regardless of my outside appearance.

I get that missing an ear is unusual and that people might need to take a second look. I'm okay with that. What I'm not okay with is when people stare, point, or whisper. I feel like they're passing judgement before getting to know me.

When this happens, I don't waste my time or energy. I either ignore it or smile and move on. If you are uncomfortable

with how I look, that is not my problem. It is your problem. That's why inclusion in advertising, entertainment, and
schools is so important. It normalizes differences. The more
you're exposed to people who are different from you, the less
you notice it.

I was fortunate to be with the same classmates from first
through eighth grades. To them I was just one of their peers
who happened to have a removable body part. They knew I
was comfortable talking about my differences and laughing if
my ear came off. It was no big deal; I could always put it back
on. These kids are now adults who are comfortable around
someone with a disability or physical difference.

Mom and I talked with my classes a few times over the
years. It was always a fun day for me to explain what a trach
and feeding tube are and why they are needed. Holding my
fake ear was fun for my classmates, and I loved shooting water
out of the feeding tube when we demonstrated how it
worked!

One thing that I never felt confident about, though, is my
hearing aid. I started struggling to keep up in second grade,
which is when the school's hearing consultant recommended
using an aid. Mom discussed this with my ENT in earlier
years, and they left it as a "wait and see" status. I hear normally
on my right side, but localizing sound is difficult.

I was also missing parts of classroom conversations despite
being positioned in the best seat to accommodate my disability. Everyone but me agreed it was time to give the hearing aid
a try. Wearing an in-ear devices was not an option because I
have no outer ear or canal.

The type of device I needed was a Cochlear Bone-Anchored Hearing Aid (BAHA). It works by vibrating the bone in my skull (bone conduction) to transmit sound. There were two options for securing the external device: 1) having a surgery to implant a post that protruded from the skin or 2) wearing a tight-fitting headband.

All the surgeries I had up to this age were medically necessary. Mom and Dad were reluctant to put me through an elective surgery. There were also potential complications with skin breakdown around the implant site.

I told them that I didn't want a post sticking out of my head. It was not that noticeable, but, in my eyes, I thought it would make me look like Frankenstein. No one pushed me to have the surgery, but without it I had to wear the BAHA on a headband.

Peter wearing his Bone-Anchored Hearing Aid (BAHA) on a headband
Photo Credit - Dede Dankelson, 2009

I hated that headband. It was itchy and embarrassing, and I took it off at any opportunity. It was "lost" on several occasions, and my teachers and Mom were in a constant battle with me about wearing it. The school provided an FM System where one piece plugged into the BAHA and my teacher wore a mic that transmitted to it.

The BAHA is expensive, and Mom spent months getting our private and supplemental state insurance to cover part of it. She was worried about it getting lost or damaged. My not wearing it was an added frustration for her.

I didn't like the responsibility of taking care of the BAHA and FM System. Sometimes my teacher would forget the microphone was on, and I could hear her talking in another room. One time I took it off during school mass because a lady was singing too loud. It disappeared for a while after that, which caused some trouble for me.

Mom had an all-points bulletin out at the church and school looking for it. I was kind of worried she might post "Lost Hearing Aid" flyers around the building. That would've been embarrassing! We eventually found it in the car door where I had stashed it after school one day.

Second grade was a tough year for me academically, but there were some fun things that happened too. Our school held an annual fundraiser, and I saw that a puppy was up for auction. I told Mom and Dad there was this cute black puppy at school, and I wanted to name him Vader.

Mom and Dad went to the auction that night with no plans to bid on the puppy. Dad was in trouble though the minute Mom saw it and found out he was a Yorkipoo breed. Dad ended up in a bidding war, which resulted in a sizeable financial contribution for the school and a cute new addition to our family.

Jacob and I were thrilled to wake up to a new puppy in the house. We went back and forth on names for a few days and Mom and Dad decided on Dexter. They were watching that show about a serial killer and thought it would be a great name for our tiny security dog.

Divot wasn't overjoyed with Dexter's arrival at first, but he warmed up to the idea of a partner in mischief. They liked to tag team us for table scraps and look for opportunities to snatch an unattended sandwich or piece of pizza.

Divot's nickname was "Garbage Goat" because he ate anything. Seriously, that dog even ate fertilizer in the garage once! Dexter is known as "Baby Cakes" and "The Boss." He's an eight-pound dude with an attitude.

Coming home to the dogs was good therapy after school. Surgeries were less frequent during my grade-school years, but I still had a lot of clinic appointments. I also had weekly speech and occupational therapy after school, and we added ortho-dontia visits to our already full schedule.

Divot and Dexter
Photo Credit - Dede Dankelson, 2010

Peter with Divot
Photo Credit - Dede Dankelson, 2010

My adult teeth came in very crooked and separated. In third grade I started calling them my "Beaver Teeth" and was embarrassed by how they looked. Mom searched for an orthodontist with craniofacial experience close to home. I was seeing the orthodontist at

Children's Hospital of Michigan in Detroit, but that was over an hour drive one way. We made that drive enough already.

Finding a new orthodontist proved easy because my pediatrician had just married a great one! She was about thirty minutes away and had experience with craniofacial patients. My "Beaver Teeth" were quickly straightened out under her care, and I felt much better about how I looked.

While my front teeth were spaced apart, my back teeth had no room because of how small my jaw was. Braces could only do so much about that. I also had four impacted teeth that needed removal. They were deep under my gums and needed to be removed by an oral surgeon.

Whenever I went into the operating room, Mom always contacted other specialists to see if there was anything they wanted to check out while I was sedated. This time was no different. ENT added a bronchoscopy and nasal endoscopy to check my upper airway.

While removing the teeth wasn't a major surgery, it was the first one I'd needed in quite a while. Mom knew my fear of the "white room" would have me stressed out for weeks leading up to the surgery. She consulted with Child Life Specialists who recommended a tour of the operating room where I could ask questions about the equipment.

We took a family trip to Children's Hospital of Michigan in Detroit where Jacob, who was four years old, participated in the tour with me. We both had a favorite stuffed animal with us as we put on surgical gowns and jumped aboard the *Surgery Express*.

I panicked as soon as we turned down the hallway toward the operating room, but we stopped just outside the door.

Peter and Jacob in an operating room at CHM, Detroit
Photo Credit - Dede Dankelson, 2010

Child Life showed me how to take slow, deep breaths to calm down. When we went through the doors and into that cold, sterile, bright room, my anxiety fully kicked in.

The Child Life Specialist was patient and waited for me to re-focus as I sat on the bed with Jacob. When I could pay attention, she explained how some of the equipment helped keep me safe during surgery. I even pretended to be Jacob's surgeon while he laid down on the bed. I liked that much better than being the patient!

What made me most anxious was the sedation mask and I.V. I hated having the mask put over my face and the smell of the anesthesia. The I.V. was inserted after I was sedated, but it freaked me out when I woke up. It was always a struggle getting me sedated because the mask would go over my mouth and nose, but I would fight it and still be breathing through the hole in my neck.

Child Life talked me through how the I.V. is inserted and showed me that the needle is only used to insert the line. What stays in your arm is more of a flexible tube. She also brought out a mask and talked about the smell. She had me pick a Chapstick flavor to rub into the mask. Jacob liked the bubblegum flavor, but I didn't care for any of it. Food and smells were not comforting to me at all.

Child Life also gave me a book to bring home. It was called *Mac Visits the Hospital* and is about a dog touring different places like surgery, radiology, the cafeteria, and exam rooms. I loved both books and dogs, and I read that story many times over the years.

Jacob stayed with a friend the day of surgery so that Mom and Dad could both be with me at the hospital. They always let me choose who went back to the operating room with me. That day was Dad's turn.

Mom and Dad both have their own trauma from these experiences. It's heartbreaking carrying your child into a scary room and watching them cry as they go under. I was nine years old for this surgery and too big to carry, so I rode on the bed.

Dad stayed in the operating room until I fell asleep. According to Mom, he looked pretty upset when he found her in the waiting room. Dad told her I was okay, but it just about killed him when I told everyone in the operating room to, "Please take good care of me" as I went under.

Mom and Dad were a little out of practice from me not having many surgeries recently, and they became anxious when the procedure lasted longer than expected. When my oral surgeon came out to speak with them, he carried a specimen jar full of teeth. In addition to the four impacted ones, he removed eight others for a total of twelve. I was getting a big pay day from the Tooth Fairy!

Everything went well with the scope of my upper airway, and nothing had changed. It was still narrow and crooked. Doctors could not get the scope down my nose or throat, so, as they'd done in previous procedures, the camera went down the hole in my neck and was flipped upward to get a view of my upper airway from below. They would still not risk closing the trach stoma.

After speaking with the surgeons, Mom and Dad waited to see me in recovery. They waited... and waited... and waited. Mom knew something wasn't right. She kept asking for updates but was told that I wasn't awake yet.

Finally, anesthesia came out and said that I was still in the PACU (post-anesthesia care unit) and having trouble breathing. They had put a trach back in and had me on a CPAP machine. CPAP stands for continuous positive airway pressure. It pushes air into your nose and mouth, helping you breathe while sleeping.

The typical process after surgery is that you go from the operating room to the PACU and then to recovery once you wake up. Parents aren't usually allowed in the PACU because patients are closely monitored and still asleep.

Mom wanted to see me for herself and was way past her breaking point. Knowing she wouldn't let up until she saw me, the hospital staff agreed to let her and Dad each have a turn in the PACU. They saw that I was on the CPAP and being closely monitored. It was hard to see the trach back in after so many years working to get rid of it.

This was supposed to be an outpatient procedure where I would go home the same day. Because of the airway complications, I was admitted for continued monitoring. When I finally got to a room, Mom asked to have the ENT on call paged. She knew from experience that I took shallow breaths while sleeping with the trach tube. It's one of the reasons I needed oxygen at night for almost the entire four years I had the trach.

I was awake by this time and very confused. I couldn't talk with the trach in and wasn't prepared for it to be there after five years without it. I also wasn't happy about spending the night in the hospital when I thought I would be going home.

Mom felt they should try removing the trach to see how I did without it. If I struggled, there was no reason it couldn't immediately be put back in. The ENT Fellow on call was getting ready to leave and did not want to come to my room. When the doctor and her bad attitude finally showed up, she didn't like Mom's idea.

Mom, of course, didn't back down. She asked why ENT had not ordered a backup trach to have at my bedside. That's standard protocol for anyone with a trach. The doctor eventually agreed to remove the tube and see how my breathing was without it. I think she realized it was the only way to appease Mom so she could go home!

As soon as the tube came out, I coughed forcefully and cleared my airway. After so much oral surgery, I had a lot of drainage that was causing blockage. I felt much better with the tube removed, and I took deeper breaths. The doctor agreed to leave the tube out with close monitoring and then happily headed home.

Dad didn't witness this entire scene. He left to get Jacob once I was in my room and awake. When he returned, I was trach free and able to talk. And the entire staff was avoiding Mom!

Jacob had never seen me after a surgery, and he was only five years old. He kept remarking that I had blood on my face. I suppose it was scary for him to see that. I told him the Tooth Fairy was going to visit me at the hospital, and that got him excited.

Dad and Jacob headed home for the night, while Mom and I set up camp in my room. We watched TV, and I asked questions about how the Tooth Fairy was going to find me. She assured me I would get a visit. After a typical sleepless night in the hospital, I woke up to a twenty-dollar bill and a note from the Tooth Fairy. She wrote how proud she was of me for being brave and that she left something else for me at home.

Jacob woke up at home to a note from the Tooth Fairy too. His note said how proud she was of him for being such a good little brother. There were also two new stuffed dogs—one for each of us. When I got home later that day, he shared one with me. It was a fun surprise, in addition to my usual welcome home from our real dog, Divot.

I didn't have any further in-patient stays for the remainder of grade school, but I did have several outpatient procedures where I was sedated. One of those was for a two-hour MRI of my head and neck because I had a few dizzy and fainting episodes that were concerning. My orthopedic surgeon said that everything still looked stable with my neck and spine curvature, but he wanted to order more tests. We consulted with neurosurgery who ordered an MRI of my brain and brain stem.

Thankfully, everything came back normal from the MRI, but we still didn't know why I was having the dizzy spells. Mom consulted with my nephrologist about my blood pressure. I started taking medication for high blood pressure when I was just a year old. It occasionally needed adjusted, but my home readings had all been good.

Sometimes there aren't any answers and issues resolve on their own. This was one of those times. The dizzy spells didn't last long and eventually went away completely. The only lasting impact was on Mom's anxiety over worrying about them.

Balancing school, therapy, and medical appointments was challenging, but not all bad. We met a lot of great people, and even had some special opportunities. Meeting Mike Babcock was one of those experiences.

Babcock was Head Coach for the Detroit Red Wings from 2005-2015, and he often invited patients from Children's Hospital of Michigan to be his guest at home games. I was one of those lucky patients.

I was about eight years old the first time I met Coach. He invited Mom and I into his office and asked me questions about why I spent so much time at the hospital. He also asked, "What do you want to be when you grow up?" I replied something about wanting to be famous. He said, "That's good. You can be what my mom taught me to be. You can be a difference maker."

I was too young to understand what that meant, but those

Peter with Coach Mike Babcock at Joe Louis Arena in Detroit
Photo Credit - Dede Dankelson, 2008

words made a big impression with Mom. She had already made it her mission in life to help other families like ours and to do whatever she could to raise awareness about craniofacial syndromes.

Mom was volunteering and raising money for Children's Craniofacial Association. She was also a Parent Advisor at Children's Hospital of Michigan in Detroit where she gave input on everything from rating the cafeteria food to how to improve discharge planning. Our family even travelled to Washington D. C. with the hospital to advocate for pediatric healthcare.

We met with state representatives and senators on behalf of the Children's Hospital Network *Speak Now for Kids* annual campaign. We shared our story about needing the Medicaid waiver for home nursing care and how much we struggled to get help. Also, we advocated for the continued support of the Graduate Medical Education Bill that encourages medical students to become pediatric specialists.

Mom was invited to occasionally speak with hospital faculty about parenting a medically complex kid. When I was about ten, she decided to start bringing me along. She taught me how to share my own experiences about being in the hospital.

Mom encouraged me to give an honest perspective, which turned out to be no problem at all. I enjoyed telling everyone in graphic detail about how blood splattered everywhere when I had labs drawn once! I also loved showing everyone my fake ear and telling stories about pranking people with it.

I did provide some helpful insights. I reminded doctors that us kids are always on high alert for key words like surgery, labs, or injections. We might look immersed in our electronics, but we're always listening. I also told them that I prefer to be told exactly what to expect before they do something to me. It eases the anxiety a little.

Mom and I also emphasized the importance of acknowledging medical PTSD. It wasn't a recognized condition then, and we wanted to make hospital staff more aware of it. I had a panic attack whenever a needle was around, and Mom would be anxious knowing it would happen. She tried multiple ways to help me manage the anxiety while simultaneously trying to control her own.

I don't think anyone truly appreciated the constant state of anxiety I lived in. I woke up every day knowing that I would need more surgeries, but I didn't know when. That unknown is a heavy burden to carry, especially when you're so young.

FOUR

Stepping Into the Spotlight

I attended St. Patrick Catholic School in White Lake, Michigan from first through eighth grade, so I did not experience moving to a different building for middle school. I was also with the same students during those years. That made middle school much less intimidating.

Having everyone familiar with my differences didn't make me stand out any more or less than someone with glasses or braces. That's what inclusion does. It reduces bullying and enables kids to grow up feeling safe and secure. My classmates were protectors, not tormentors.

Socially I was always included in activities at school and welcomed into groups. By middle school, though, most of my classmates were involved in sports and clubs that did not interest me. Because of all my time in hospitals and recovering from surgeries, I didn't mature on a typical timeframe.

Fantasy play was my escape from constant anxiety. It was great in second and third grade when everyone played light sabers at recess. By late elementary, though, my friends started growing out of pretend play.

Star Wars was always my favorite, but I also liked *Harry Potter* and *Lego Bionics*. I was also somewhat obsessed with dogs. Even in middle school, my favorite books to read were about dogs. I had a stuffed animal version of just about every dog breed and always took one with me to the hospital. They were a good substitute since Divot could not come to my appointments.

Jacob, being four years younger, bridged the gap as my peers outgrew role playing. He and I had some great after-school and weekend adventures playing super-heroes and having light saber duels. I was sad when Jacob eventually lost interest too.

It was frustrating for me that everyone outgrew the fantasy play. I spent a lot of time building Lego sets and collecting *Star Wars* figures well into middle school. I also loved books and, of course, hanging out with Divot and Dexter.

My parents worked hard trying to find age-appropriate activities that would get me involved in a social group. I tried piano and karate lessons and was in Cub Scouts for a while, but none of those activities held my interest. Sports did not appeal to me either, which was kind of a good thing.

I can't play contact sports because of a single, pelvic kidney and the instability of my neck. I was also unable to swim underwater because I still had the hole in my neck. Even though the tube came out when I was four, the hole (stoma) never closed on its own.

Doctors would not surgically close the stoma, knowing they would need it for future surgeries. Whenever I needed to be sedated, they would put a trach tube back in to secure my airway. This was the safest thing for me, but it meant that I still couldn't go swimming.

Tumbling, trampolines, and roller coasters were other activities I was told to avoid because of potential instability with my neck. For a while it seemed like I was constantly hearing, "You can't do anything fun."

These restrictions were separating me more and more from my peers. Think about how many birthday parties are at pools or trampoline parks. It was a constant reminder that I was different.

Something else that always made me feel different was being pulled out of class to work with special education teachers. I did not like being singled out from everyone else. It magnified my differences and that is not something any middle schooler wants! I also hated having to make up work because of missing class time.

I struggled with organization, study skills, and the faster pace of middle school. It was exhausting to keep up both for me and Mom. Dad travelled a lot, so she spent hours helping me with homework.

Mom believed I had an undiagnosed learning disability and hoped that testing might reveal ways to help me in school. After consulting with our pediatrician, she arranged for me to have a private neuropsychology test.

I was in sixth grade and twelve years old when Mom took me for this appointment. She made sure I was well rested and understood that the testing was to help me in school. Unfortunately, it wasn't at all helpful. It was actually pretty devastating for all of us.

After a day of testing, I was left alone in the lobby while the psychiatrist spent two hours in a private conversation with my parents. When they finally emerged, Mom was crying, and Dad didn't look too good either. This doctor was adamant that I would never become a productive, functioning adult.

She repeatedly emphasized her Harvard education while offering no constructive advice on how to help me in school. During one point in the conversation, the doctor even went so far as to tell my parents they should stop trying so hard with me and accept that my brother would be their only "normal" child.

Here is some advice from a lot of experience. When a doctor starts speaking in absolutes and thinks they have a crystal ball, don't walk out of their office. RUN! My parents were in such shock that they failed to do that. It took them time to recover from that meeting and to realize that this specialist was very wrong.

My teachers encouraged Mom and Dad to get another opinion because the findings from this psychiatrist were so different from previous testing I had done at school. Mom, somewhat reluctantly, took me to another pediatric specialist who was also confounded with the first results. His testing aligned more with the school's findings. In the end, everyone agreed to trash the "Harvard Crystal Ball Report."

The neuropsychology testing left us emotionally drained. Mom still had no good advice on how to help me in school. My parents knew I would get more support through the public school, but they knew how much I loved my teachers and peers. They didn't want to take me out of that familiar environment. I'm glad they didn't move me because I loved my time at St. Patrick School.

Despite all my medical restrictions, Mom and Dad made sure I safely participated in as many parties and field trips as I could. They both pushed me in different ways and had different ideas about what was an acceptable risk. I quickly learned which parent to go to depending on the activity.

Mom's always been fearful of me in the water, but she agreed I could be in the pool if I used a circular float. That worked well when I was younger, and everyone played in the kiddie pools. It became embarrassing as I got older, and all my friends were diving into the deep end and doing hand stands underwater.

I like to push the limits, and I knew Dad would take more risks with me in the water. He was always my "go to parent" for all things water related. Mom preferred to not know about our shenanigans.

She always said, "If I don't know about it, it didn't happen!" We've taken many beach and lake-side family vacations. I went tubing, kayaking, parasailing, and white-water rafting with the open airway. Pairing me with Dad on these excursions worked best for all of us!

Mom was better equipped for other activities. My fifth-grade class did an overnight field trip that included a zip line and high-ropes course. The school said I could not participate without a parent present. Dad has a fear of heights, so Mom took on that one.

She made sure I didn't miss out on any of the experience, and my classmates cheered me on as I did the high-ropes course. It was challenging and made me feel proud that I completed the obstacles. I am grateful to have that memory of accomplishment vs one of watching from the sidelines.

The roller coaster restriction was a huge downer because I love riding them. It was something I had been allowed to do and then had to stop. Fortunately, it was only for a few years.

As Mom and Dad gained more experience communicating with my specialists, they learned that doctors tend to make broad statements like, "no riding roller coasters." There is often some room for a safe compromise. My parents learned to respectfully ask questions, so they acquired a better understanding to assess my risk in various activities.

What they learned is that I should not ride a coaster that might whip my neck quickly forward or backward. Understanding this made them comfortable allowing me to ride coasters with high-back seats that would support my neck. With the doctors in agreement, I was eventually back on the tracks fueling my adrenaline rush.

Listening to my parents discuss these issues with doctors taught me how to advocate for myself. Life is not to be lived in a bubble; it is full of risks. The key to living your best life is learning which risks are worth taking.

Summer breaks during my middle school years were sometimes lonely. Without school or a regular activity, I didn't have much daily interaction with peers. We were always busy, but my parents worried that I spent too much time alone. Mom's solution was day camps.

When I was around twelve years old, she signed me up for one of those dreaded weeks. I didn't know any kids at this camp, but I made a few friends the first day. There was also this kid that wouldn't stop staring at me. I felt his negative vibe and tried to stay away from him, but he just couldn't see past my differences.

We were on the playground one afternoon, and he stopped me from crossing over on the bridge. He blocked me and said, "You're weird. Everything about you is weird: your ear, your neck, the way you eat, the way you talk." I was intimidated and taken by surprise.

I turned around and walked away, playing the role of victim. What he said hurt, but it also made me angry. I thought, "he doesn't know anything about me!" That afternoon I watched him continue being a bully to other kids, and I grew angrier.

When I saw him alone on the swings, I walked up, looked him in the eye, and said, "You know what? You're a jerk!" I walked away that second time feeling empowered and strong. It was his turn to be speechless, and he stopped bullying kids the rest of the week.

Sometimes you need to take a stand, not just for you but others as well. It's scary and takes courage. Grab a friend who feels the same as you and call someone out together. If you're a kid, ask a trusted adult for advice.

I constantly edit people out of my thoughts by ignoring stares and whispers. Those are the day-to-day moments that can stack up and eventually fall right on top of you. People have called me weird and creepy. They've tried to touch my little ear or sat uncomfortably close on a dare.

As I've said, I get that my appearance might cause a second look. That's okay. What you do after that second glance though says more about you than me. I know when you're staring, and I see when you whisper and point. That's not okay.

Although I'm still not a fan of summer camps, I did learn there are benefits to being the outsider. Sounds terrifying, I know, but hear me out. If you have the courage to be yourself, you automatically have a filter that attracts genuine friends and repels those who are insincere.

Humor has always been the easiest way for me to handle an awkward situation. I used to tell kids, "I don't bite!" or "Don't worry, your ear won't fall off. I was just born without one." If I acknowledge it and let people know I'm comfortable with how I look, they are more likely to relax and get to know the real me.

As you can imagine, I had a lot of fun pranking people with my prosthetic ear. I'd let it hang halfway off my head after a sweaty gym class or leave it in a desk for someone to find. The reactions were always priceless!

I'm not advocating that you make fun of yourself. There's a difference between getting people to laugh with you vs laugh at you. You can tell the difference by if it makes you feel good about yourself. Genuinely laughing together is a great way to connect and leaves everyone feeling good.

I think that's a big reason my family felt so connected to the fictional story in *Wonder* by R.J. Palacio. Mom read the book just after it was published in early 2012. She loved how relatable it was to our own experience.

The book is about a ten-year-old boy with a craniofacial syndrome and his first year transitioning from home to private school. I was about the same age as the fictional character,

Peter with Dexter and the book Wonder by R.J. Palacio
Photo Credit - Dede Dankelson, 2012

Auggie, and we had a lot more than just the medical condition
in common.

We were both *Star Wars* fans, loved our dogs, went to a

private school, wore a hearing aid, and had one sibling. Even our birthdays were close, just three days apart! The way the family used humor to cope with daily issues also resonated with mine.

As the book gained popularity in schools, a few of Mom's teacher friends asked if I would be comfortable speaking with their students. They liked how I was able to bring the fictional story to life, and students loved learning about all my cool equipment. I even let them hold one of my fake ears!

Mom introduced the book to her colleagues on Children's Craniofacial Association's Board of Directors and presented it as an opportunity to educate the public about facial differences. She envisioned other CCA kids speaking at schools and sharing what it's really like to live with a craniofacial syndrome.

CCA's Board embraced this idea and launched the #ChooseKind Education and Outreach program. They provided *Wonder* books to schools with curriculum materials. They also developed the "Meet a Real-Life Auggie" program, connecting teachers with a CCA Kid. Students were able to ask questions and learn more about facial differences through either a video call or an in-person visit.

The book even became a popular community read. In 2013, I portrayed Auggie in a staged reading for Santa Monica Public Library's *One Book, One Community* program. I received a script to practice from home and then flew to California for the show.

Actor and Director, Edward Edwards, staged the rehearsals and production. It was fun meeting professional actors and kids from the local acting school. One of the

Peter and Jacob in Santa Monica, California
Photo Credit - Dede Dankelson, 2013

highlights for me was getting a standing ovation for my performance!

The author, R.J. Palacio, flew in for the show, so I was able to thank her in person for writing such an amazing story. I even signed books with her after the performance!

As *Wonder* climbed the bestseller lists, Coach Babcock invited me to be his guest at another Detroit Red Wings game. Dad went with me this time, and we gave him a copy of *Wonder*. I told Coach how I was speaking at schools about the importance of kindness and inclusion. We let him know that his earlier advice to "Be a Difference Maker" had become a motto for our family.

Peter with Coach Mike Babcock at Joe Louis Arena in Detroit
Photo Credit - Darin Dankelson, 2013

Coach loved the story, and he gave me a book too. His book is called *Leave No Doubt: A Credo for Chasing Your Dreams*. It's a story about the importance of mindset and mental grit in sports and in life. The book shares a credo that Babcock and his coaching staff wrote for the 2010 Olympics when they were under intense pressure to bring home the gold for Canada.

I've read the book several times, and I'm guessing Mom has read it even more. It's a quick but impactful read about determination, commitment, and how to achieve your dreams. I was in middle school when I met with Coach the second time, so I remember it better.

His words not only inspired me to make a difference through speaking. They also made me realize how one small act of kindness, like inviting a kid to a hockey game and having a quick conversation, has the power to impact countless lives.

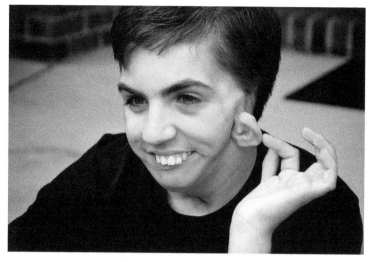

Peter being silly with his prosthetic ear
Photo Credit - Images by Marie Moore, 2015

Wonder went on to become a worldwide bestseller, giving the craniofacial community a sense of pride and social acceptance that had never existed. It gave kids like me a hero we could look up to. I loved showing students that being different is cool and nothing to be afraid of.

I brought props with me to presentations, and let kids pass them around while I spoke. They learned that a trach is just a different way to breathe, a feeding tube is just a different way to eat, and a hearing aid is just a different way to hear. They got a close look at my prosthetic ear and learned how it was made.

Mom and I noticed that students were focused on my differences in the beginning of a presentation, but, by the end, they were asking questions about my favorite foods and movies. They had already learned to look past my disabilities. They just wanted to know more about me.

Students could easily connect with me about having either a sibling or a pet, so I usually talked about both. Like Auggie's dog, Daisy, Divot was my confidant and best friend. I always had a picture of Divot in my presentations.

Unfortunately, I also had the same experience as Auggie when Divot became ill one night. He was twelve years old, and I had to say goodbye to him the next day. I was devastated and heartbroken. I will always be grateful for his unconditional love and companionship. He was my best friend.

Fortunately, I still had Dexter to hang out with. Dexter, however, had never been without his buddy, and we noticed he was getting into more mischief than usual. He obviously needed a new partner in crime.

While there was no replacing Divot, we did eventually add a new member to the family. Abby is a crazy, lovable miniature labradoodle that makes us laugh every day. Sometimes I think she channels Divot's mischief but in her own, unique way.

As middle school came to a close, my parents struggled with what high school I should attend. Many of my classmates were heading to a private school, but Mom and Dad knew I would receive more disability services through the public high school.

Dad was traveling even more during my last year of middle school, and he and Mom began thinking about an out of state move. Dad was spending almost every week in Illinois and Wisconsin. He didn't like missing so many of our activities and family time together.

The move to Illinois was inevitable for Dad's work, but it was his decision on when to do it. Much to my dismay, they decided to make the move before I started high school. I was mad, but there wasn't much I could do about it.

Mom and Dad felt it was the best time because everyone in my class would be transitioning to a new school. Some would stay together, but many would not. They also knew that even if some of my classmates went to the same high school, I might not be in any of the same classes. Moving out of state made it a bit more intimidating, but I would be starting over regardless.

Before the school year ended, we spent a week in Illinois looking at houses and schools for me and Jacob. I was intimidated by the big buildings and crowded hallways. All the high schools we toured were around the same size, but there was one that stood out for me.

The student who gave me the tour of Libertyville High School was really excited about it. He made me feel like LHS was the place for me, and his enthusiasm was contagious. I started thinking I might survive the move after all.

Mom and Dad also liked Libertyville, and we found a house just a few miles from the high school. Jacob's school was even closer. He started fifth grade at St. Joseph Catholic School in Libertyville. With that all settled, we started packing for a summer move.

Dankelson Family at home in Michigan
Photo Credit - Images by Marie Moore, 2015

FIVE

Overcoming Adversity with a Guitar

We moved to Illinois in July, so I had about a month to get used to our new neighborhood. Mom took me to register at the high school, and we both got our exercise walking through my schedule and finding classrooms. I was both excited and scared about the start of school.

One of the hardest parts of moving for me was the loss of a familiar community. I felt comfortable at school and in our neighborhood where everyone knew my medical story. Moving meant meeting people who were not familiar with me. It meant more stares and whispers.

Walking into the building on the first day was so intimidating. I was a little freshman and there were dudes with full beards in the hallways! What a culture shock coming from my small, private school where everyone wore the same uniform every day.

My main objective was to stay under the radar and not get stuffed into a locker. I gratefully achieved that and made it to most of my classes on time. Lunch was terrifying, but some guys invited me to sit with them. They were also freshman but knew each other from middle school.

I couldn't follow much of what was being said at the lunch table, so I just smiled and nodded a lot. Having single-sided hearing makes it difficult to have conversations in loud places like the cafeteria. There's no way I was going to say, "Can you please repeat that. My left ear is fake, and I can't hear on that side."

As a freshman, I didn't have my hearing implant yet, and I wore the prosthetic ear every day to hold up my glasses. Of course, it also prevented unwanted stares, which is exactly what I wanted. So, I survived my first day of high school without any major incidents. I successfully blended in—or so I thought.

As the school year kicked in, I became less intimidated. My favorite class first semester was called Link Crew where freshman attend a lunch meeting with upper class leaders who mentored us about all things social and academic. One of the leaders was a football player who encouraged me to come to the first home game.

Mom and Dad thought it was great that I wanted to go to the game, but they were concerned that I wasn't going with a group. I told them I was meeting kids in the student section. When we got to the stadium, Dad left me at the student gate alone and pulled Mom toward the guest entrance.

She was panicked that I was by myself. Jacob finds friends everywhere, so he immediately saw kids from his new school and stayed with them. Mom and Dad found a spot in the stands. Dad enjoyed the game, while Mom stressed about how I was doing.

Mom felt better when they saw me walking with a group of boys. At halftime, I texted her to find out where they were sitting. I had had my fill of the student section. It was loud and crowded, and I couldn't hear a thing. So much noise coming at me all at once was exhausting and overwhelming.

I sat with Mom and Dad for the third quarter and was telling them that my Link Crew leader was #44. Mom couldn't believe it. My Uncle played football in high school and that was his number. My guardian angel was still with me.

That was one of only a few times I went to a high school football game. Throughout the years, I went to other games, but it was always too noisy and difficult to connect with people. While I loved the excitement of it all, it just wasn't fun for me.

I eventually began to relax at school and let others know I had a sense of humor about my differences. After making a few friends, I realized that being okay with how I looked made it easier to meet people. I was never going to blend in and trying to hide that I had Goldenhar Syndrome only made me look insecure.

I was more comfortable with people at school knowing the real me. I did not feel like I was hiding this big secret anymore. Still, it took time to find my place socially.

I didn't really fit in with the athletic, drama, or art groups, although I was friendly with many students who were involved in those activities. I was reluctant to join the special needs clubs because I wasn't sure where I fit there either. I wanted to be part of something, but I was scared to take a step in any specific direction.

There was a student in my math class who I connected

with because we liked the same video games. We talked a few times before class, and he invited me over one weekend. Instead of gaming as I expected, he wanted to go to the mall and hang out with some sketchy kids. They were all into drinking and smoking. I quickly figured out that he was more interested in "recruiting" me to be part of this group than being my friend.

The next time he invited me to hang out, I told him, "I deal with enough already. I don't need to do stupid stuff for attention." So, that friendship basically ended before it even got started. I'm glad I trusted my instincts and did not invest further time with this kid. He really was bad news.

The first club I tried was Fencing. My parents thought I would love it because of my affinity for dueling with light sabers! And, how cool was it that my high school had a fencing club? I didn't appreciate it at the time, but attending Libertyville High School was one of the best things that came from our move to Illinois. LHS has a club for EVERYTHING. In fact, I think they are recognized for it.

I enjoyed Fencing Club, especially the coaches. They were very encouraging, but it was a big commitment. We practiced three to four nights a week and had tournaments on the weekends. I didn't like spending my entire Saturday at the competitions. I sat around waiting several hours for a chance to duel just once or twice. The tournaments were also very loud.

My teammates enjoyed hanging out all day. I struggled with the noise and chaotic environment. My hearing loss made situations like that exhausting.

I finished the season my freshman year, but it just never lit a fire inside me. That's okay because about three months after the season ended, I found something that did. That's when I picked up a guitar for the first time.

Music was a big part of how I coped with moving out of state and starting high school. It started in eighth grade with listening to hits that were popular with my peers and played at school dances. Those were primarily pop songs.

Hearing "Eruption" by Van Halen for the first time is what got me listening to more rock music. I still remember the first time I heard it. I was about fourteen years old and in the car with Dad. "Eruption" came on, and he said, "You need to hear this."

Listening to Van Halen led me to AC/DC. That's when I started thinking about playing guitar. I mentioned it to Dad one night toward the end of my freshman year, and he said, "Well, you're in luck. I happen to have one in the basement."

Dad still had a Fender electric guitar and bass he played in high school. We pulled them out of storage, along with a Peavey Amp. Dad showed me the basics of how everything worked and left me to explore and play it on my own.

I started searching YouTube for guitar instruction and found a lot of great teachers. For over a year, I was happy learning what interested me and going at my own pace. My first obsession was studying Malcolm and Angus Young. That was followed by Guns N' Roses and Slash.

I got frustrated a few times, but I never gave up. I have a hypoplastic left thumb, which means it's not functional. There is no muscle, and it doesn't bend. I can't grip anything with that hand or use it when playing guitar. That's my fretting hand, so I had to get creative with ways to use only four fin-

Peter with his Dad's Fender Musicmaster
Photo Credit - Dede Dankelson, 2016

gers. The issue with my thumb only made me try harder. I was determined to learn.

I'm glad my parents didn't push me to take lessons right away. Exploring on my own was like therapy. I loved immersing myself in learning a new song, technique, or effect. It is still the way I prefer to learn, even though I may have picked up some unusual habits.

People often notice I hold the guitar pick between my thumb and middle finger instead of the traditional thumb and index finger. I had no idea when I was starting out that

Eddie Van Halen held a pick the same way. Some wonder if I learned that from watching EVH, but I had no idea until much later.

As my excitement with the guitar grew, I became interested in hearing better. Mom and I had many appointments after our move. I still needed regular check-ups with the ENT for airway and hearing, nephrology for my single-pelvic kidney, orthopedics for my back and neck, ophthalmology for my vision, and orthodontia in preparation for future jaw surgery.

Dr. Michael Shinners, one of the ENT doctors we met with, specialized in hearing implants, and asked me about the Bone-Anchored Hearing Aid (BAHA). After continuing to fight about it during middle school, Mom had completely given up on making me use it.

We learned there was a new method of securing the outer device called the Cochlear BAHA Attract System. That intrigued me because by then I was old enough to understand how much this device could help me.

The implant worked the same by implanting a screw in the skull to generate bone conduction. The difference was how the external device attached through a magnet implanted under the skin on top of the bone screw. This eliminated the need to have a post sticking out of my head. It also meant less daily maintenance and lower risk of infection.

I knew that I was missing parts of conversations and being in a larger school made this more obvious to me. When the doctor mentioned it had a Bluetooth feature, I was even more intrigued. I agreed to try a loaner on the headband after Mom said she wouldn't make me wear it at school.

Mom suggested I try it out at home and maybe a few

louder environments. Our deal was that I would be honest about if I liked it, but there would be no pressure to have the surgery or wear it on the headband once the trial was over.

When wearing the BAHA loaner at home, I realized how much it helped me follow conversations and hear the TV. What I loved most was the Bluetooth feature. I could stream music and videos directly from my iPhone to the device.

Mom talked me into trying it at a movie theater where I could wear it without being noticed. That was incredible. It was the closest I had ever come to hearing surround sound. Still, I was afraid to have the surgery.

Mom and Dad said the decision was entirely up to me. They didn't pressure me either way but gave their opinion if I asked. Mom said she would help me get answers to questions about the surgery and recovery. I took my time weighing the pros and cons and working mentally through the fear.

I was relieved it was an outpatient procedure, so I didn't need to stay overnight in the hospital. It's what I call a "stitch and go." I also liked that the external device now attached with a magnet instead of the post. The main benefit, of course, was hearing better. I must admit though, the Bluetooth feature is what really convinced me to go through with it!

When I finally decided to have the surgery, we all agreed that summer break would be the best time to schedule it. So, after finishing my first year of high school, I had surgery for the Cochlear BAHA Attract implant.

I was re-thinking that decision in pre-op, but I had three things helping me out: 1) Mom & Dad, 2) anti-anxiety meds, and 3) AC/DC. Dr. Shinners and the NorthShore medical team even cranked up "Highway to Hell" as they wheeled me back to the operating room!

The surgery went well, and I was home recovering within the same day. I had minimal pain and even went to an outdoor concert a day after the surgery. It was my first concert since picking up a guitar, and the Steve Miller Band did not disappoint. Thankfully, I only had to wear a large bandage on my head for twenty-four hours, so I was only sporting a shaved haircut and dressing over the incision. Very rock and roll!

Peter wearing his hearing aid
Photo Credit - Dede Dankelson, 2016

After a month of healing, I received the external device. Mom and I went to the audiologist's office to have the BAHA activated and programmed. The settings were customized for my hearing needs, and there are different strengths of magnets to try out. You want the device to be secure, but not too tight that it causes skin breakdown.

I've been using the BAHA daily for more than five years and haven't had any complications. It's honestly the best decision I've ever made for myself. To say it was life changing is an understatement. I will not go a day without wearing it. Mom realized how important it was when I begged her to bring it to me at school one morning when I forgot to put it on.

It does draw attention and second glances, but I don't care. In fact, I'm proud of the BAHA and keep my hair short to show it off. Plus, I now have a magnet implanted in my head and, as you can imagine, I have some fun party tricks.

Not too long after I was fully healed, I started wondering about the magnetic implant. Before the surgery, we asked about going through airport security and complications if I needed an MRI. The doctor said there would be no issues with any of that. It got me thinking though that I might be able to stick something magnetic to my head.

Fridge magnets were easily accessible, so I held a few close to where the magnet was implanted. Sure enough, they stuck! Mom held a spoon close to my head and could feel the magnetic pull. It was too heavy to stick though.

Peter being silly with an eyeball magnet
Photo Credit - Dede Dankelson, 2016

I'm always on the lookout for funny magnets. One year for Halloween I walked around school with an eyeball magnet on the side of my head. You can imagine the looks that got. Key chains are fun too!

Choosing to wear the BAHA means I value what is best for me more than what someone else might think. Deciding to have the surgery gave me another layer of confidence. That is what happens when you repeatedly make decisions that are in your own best interest. It fuels you with the courage to do hard things.

I started my second year of high school wearing the BAHA and streaming music through it between classes. Okay, I admittedly listened to music sometimes during class. I usually kept it quiet enough to get away with, but there was the occasion it was heard by a teacher.

I had also joined two clubs: Best Buddies and Young Life. Best Buddies is a mentoring club where students with intellectual disabilities are paired with a buddy. What I enjoyed about Best Buddies was that it offered an inclusive group that was all about good times and supporting each other.

Our Best Buddies Club often attended school functions together. That made it easier and fun to participate in social events like homecoming and prom. We attended as a group and did not feel the pressure to find a date or go alone.

They also hosted an annual talent show, and that's the first opportunity I had to play for an audience. I practiced for weeks and was so excited. I had the entire gym floor to myself and played "Detroit Rock City," by Kiss. It was fun because everyone knew and loved the song. That gave me a taste for wanting to do more live performances.

The other club I found was Young Life, which is a non-denominational Christian youth group that meets outside of school. We met on Monday nights, and it was always a good time. Many of the same students from Best Buddies were also part of Young Life, and I made some great friendships.

I had a busy schedule that year between homework, clubs, and speaking at schools, but I always found time to practice guitar. I spent three to four hours many nights playing and learning everything I could from YouTube videos.

Wonder's popularity continued to grow, and Hollywood announced it would be made into a family movie. After that announcement, we were inundated with speaking requests. Mom had to limit my speaking engagements to one to two per week so that I wouldn't miss too much school.

Mom never charged a speaker's fee for our presentations. Instead, she asked for a non-specific donation to Children's Craniofacial Association. We didn't want to turn a school down if they did not have funding for a speaker, but we did want CCA to be recognized. CCA provided the curriculum materials free of charge, and we volunteered our time and travel. It was championing inclusion and kindness in schools, and we were happy to be part of it.

WGN News in Chicago ran a story about our presentations. They filmed parts of a school assembly and interviewed us about our connection to the book, thoughts on the up-

Peter speaking at a school assembly
Photo Credit - Dede Dankelson, 2017

coming movie, and our involvement with Children's Cranio-facial Association.

We also traveled to California my sophomore year, where I was honored as a Champion of Hope by Global Genes. They hosted a gala event to recognize people making a difference in the rare disease community. I was unknowingly nominated for the award by Erica Klauber, CCA's Executive Director.

Peter and Jacob with Travis Lively and Geoff Reeves
Photo Credit - Dede Dankelson, 2016

Before the Gala, Global Genes wanted to know who my heroes were. I said, "the men and women who serve our country and protect our freedoms." So, they invited two real-life Navy SEALs to present me with the award.

Geoff Reeves and Travis Lively honored me with their SEAL team challenge coins and a signed SEAL flag. A challenge coin is a small medallion or coin that reflects membership in a unit, team, or mission. Receiving a SEAL team member's challenge coin is a sign of honor and respect. Geoff and Travis said I was their hero because I wear my armor every day. I can never take it off.

They also said that SEALs never work alone. They always have a buddy. That's when they invited my brother up to the stage and recognized him for being a Super Sibling. Marcus Luttrell, Navy SEAL and author of *Lone Survivor*, sent us a signed copy of his book and autographed boots from The Boot Campaign. It was an incredible honor and brought more opportunities my way.

Harmony 4 Hope is a charity that leverages the power of music to unite people in the rare disease community. Their Executive Director, Kerry Hughes, learned about me from the Global Genes Gala. Kerry found out we lived in the Chicago area and reached out to Mom about getting involved.

One of Harmony 4 Hope's programs is called Rare Storytellers where they invite people in the rare disease community to share patient stories. As a Rare Storyteller for H4H, I've had the opportunity to share my journey at Northwestern's Feinberg School of Medicine, Marquette University's College of Health Sciences, and Medical College of Wisconsin's College of Health Sciences.

Those events also connected me with Harmony 4 Hope's music ambassador, Trapper Schoepp. Trapper is a singer/songwriter based in Milwaukee, Wisconsin. In addition to sharing my story with medical students, H4H gave me the opportunity to play with Trapper at these events.

Peter with Trapper Schoepp at a Harmony 4 Hope Event
Photo Credit – Jesse Lee, Marquette University, 2018

Most of the Rare Storyteller events were in the evening, so I didn't need to miss more school to participate. My high school, though, was very accommodating with my schedule. They allowed us to book Q & A video calls with classes during my lunch breaks. The District 128 School Board even invited me to speak to them about the #ChooseKind movement and my involvement with *Wonder*.

Casting for the *Wonder* movie kept everyone excited about the book. The buzz really increased when it was announced that Julia Roberts and Owen Wilson would be portraying the parents. There was a lot of debate about who should play Auggie.

Some, especially within the craniofacial community, wanted a kid with a real facial difference to portray the character. I agree it would've been exciting to have Hollywood do a search for an actor with a craniofacial syndrome. They chose not to do that search though once Jacob Tremblay agreed to portray Auggie.

Tremblay had become recognized for his role in the movie, *Room,* starring Brie

Peter and Jacob with Jacob Tremblay at a CCA Retreat
Photo Credit - Dede Dankelson, 2016

Larsen who won an Academy Award for Best Actress. Even though he didn't have a craniofacial syndrome, he had proven himself to be a good actor. I felt that was just as important.

In preparation for filming, Jacob and his family attended CCA's 2016 retreat. Interacting with so many Real Wonders gave him good insight on how to represent Auggie. His family wanted to make sure he connected with kids within the craniofacial community, and CCA welcomed them into our tribe.

The producers wanted more of the cast to meet *Wonder* kids and invited several CCA families, including mine, to visit the movie set in Vancouver. It was a fun experience seeing how the movie scenes were shot and learning how the makeup crew transformed Tremblay's face every day using prosthetics.

It took two hours every morning to alter Tremblay's appearance and another hour to remove the makeup after filming wrapped for the day. I noticed they used the same adhesive as me, and I showed the artists my own prosthetic ear.

We also visited the costume and props trailers. I got to try on Auggie's helmet, and the props manager showed me it had a microphone in it. He showed us the light sabers used in the movie, and I, of course, had to hold one.

The *Wonder*-related fun was a good distraction from my impending jaw surgery. I had known about "The Big One" my entire life, but I never knew exactly when or how it would happen. Mom and Dad didn't either. What they did know is that my jaw had not grown since distraction when I was three. It was recessed and once again obstructing my airway.

Here's the best way I know to describe why I couldn't breathe normally. Pinch your nose closed and stick your tongue to the roof of your mouth. Now, try to breathe in through your mouth. You can't because your tongue is blocking your upper airway.

That is why I needed the trach at birth, and that is why I still had the open hole in my neck. The early surgeries lengthened my jaw enough to remove the trach, but my bones did not grow. By the time I was fifteen, I was almost completely reliant on breathing through my neck again.

Chewing and swallowing was also becoming difficult. I had such an extreme overbite that I couldn't even touch my tongue to my front teeth. I found a new orthodontist as soon as we moved to Illinois, and, by the end of my first year of high school, I had a second round of braces in my mouth.

My new orthodontist and pediatrician helped Mom set up consults with prospective jaw surgeons. She wanted multiple opinions. Dr. Arlene Rozzelle, my craniofacial surgeon from Children's Hospital of Michigan, strongly recommended one specific doctor. Mom was resisting this recommendation because the surgeon had just moved from Illinois to Michigan—the exact opposite of us. She preferred to stay in-state, but she valued Dr. Rozzelle's opinion.

Our first consults were with a craniofacial practice in Illinois who ordered new CT scans. Those scans were then sent to the out of state surgeon, Dr. John Polley, who offered his expertise on the phone. It came down to two options: 1) another jaw distraction to lengthen my jaw followed by a second procedure called a Le Fort or 2) mandibular reconstruction with a Le Fort osteotomy and tempo-mandibular joint (TMJ) implant.

As with anything, there were pros and cons to both. The TMJ implant was a newer procedure with less long-term data. I had already been through jaw distraction as a toddler, and it had been mildly successful. The problem with distraction is that you can't control direction of the bone growth, and quality of the new bone, at least in my experience, wasn't good.

Distraction also involves multiple surgeries to place and remove the device.

After many conversations with my parents, meetings with surgeons, and input from Mom doing her investigative work with other parents, I decided to go with the TMJ Implant. It was a hard decision and gave me a glimpse of what Mom and Dad went through when I was younger. There are no absolutes in medicine, just opinions based on varying degrees of expertise and experience.

Once I made the decision, we embarked on a year of planning and preparation. The primary experts throughout the process were my orthodontist, Dr. Lee Graber in Vernon Hills, Illinois and my craniofacial surgeons, Drs. John Polley and John Girotto, at Helen DeVos Children's Hospital in Grand Rapids, Michigan. Their ability to collaborate and communicate effectively was key to my successful outcome, and I remain grateful that they excelled at it.

The first step on my jaw reconstruction journey was starting a second round of braces. My teeth needed to be moved into position before the surgery. I also had a surgery where fat was taken from my thigh and grafted around where the TMJ implant would eventually be placed. Once my teeth were close to position, updated CT scans were ordered. Those scans were used to make 3D bone models of my jaw that were then used to design the implant.

The surgical team used those models and scans to simulate my surgery. This enabled them to foresee complications before I was in the operating room. Several things came up during this process. My surgeons, for example, intended to use plates and screws to lengthen my right (non-implant) side.

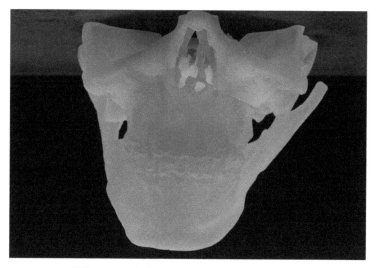

3D bone model of Peter's jaw before reconstruction
Photo Credit - Chris Clark, Spectrum Health Beat, 2017

During the simulation, they discovered that I did not have enough bone to do that.

Dr. Polley updated us with this issue and said he would need to harvest bone from my skull to graft on the right side. A neurosurgeon would do the skull graft, and I would have more incision sites. While this was not great news, it's certainly better to find out before the surgery.

TMJ Concepts, the company that designed my implant, is in Ventura, California. A few months before surgery, Mom contacted them about touring their facility. We were in California to speak at schools, and she thought it would be interesting to learn how they make the implant.

Mom also knew that making a connection with the people designing my implant would personalize it for them. I would not just be a name or number on the assembly line. This turned out to be very beneficial because they nicknamed my case, "Mr. Impossible."

Had they not made a personal connection with me, the designers may have given up. They were finding it impossible (hence the nickname) to design an implant that could be safely secured to my existing bone structure. Dr. Polley was not comfortable with any of the designs they presented him with, so he began to consider other options.

If they could not use my existing anatomy, I would need bone grafted to create a structure for the implant to adhere. This would mean two surgeries six months apart, instead of one surgery at the beginning of the summer. It was devastating news. We had been planning for over a year and my surgery was a month away when this bad news dropped.

We spent an anxious week waiting as Dr. Polley took a much-needed vacation and the engineers at TMJ Concepts continued to work on design ideas. This was the week that Mom's stress level exceeded all limits. Picture a pressure cooker exploding, and you'll have a good idea of what Mom looked like that week. Dad and I like to tease her about how stressed out she gets, but, in all seriousness, that is a big part of why I stay mentally strong. I don't want my parents worrying about my mental state on top of everything else.

Unable to get in touch with Dr. Polley, Mom contacted TMJ Concepts directly. They were helpful in answering some of her questions. That lowered her blood pressure a bit. I got through all the uncertainty by immersing myself in playing guitar and listening to music.

Dr. Polley contacted us from the airport on his return home. TMJ Concepts had sent him a new design. Their en-

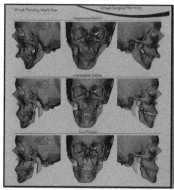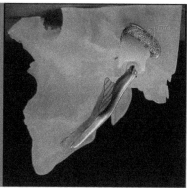

Computer generated TMJ implant on Peter Dankelson's 3D bone model
Photo Credit - Chris Clark, Spectrum Health Beat, 2017

gineers proposed adhering the implant from underneath the bone versus the traditional method of on top of the bone.

Dr. Polley wanted to spend his weekend reviewing the new design, but he thought it looked very promising. He said he would call on Monday with a final decision. Thank goodness for creative engineers at TMJ Concepts because we received good news on Monday that the surgery was back on.

Less than a month later, I was on the road to Grand Rapids, Michigan for my biggest surgery to date. Mom and I drove together, and Dad and Jacob followed in a separate car. As we passed the Welcome to Michigan sign, I looked up and saw an eagle fly over us across the highway. It was surreal and comforting to see that magnificent bird. I knew then that my angel, Uncle Justin, would help me through this difficult surgery and recovery. Uncle Justin loved eagles, and seeing one always reminds us of him. I believe "God Winks" are out there if you pay attention.

After the four-hour drive, we checked into the hospital hotel and went together to my pre-op appointments at Helen DeVos Children's Hospital. I had to meet the neurosurgeon who would be taking a bone graft from my skull, the ENT who would be securing my airway, and check-in with Dr. Polley and Dr. Girotto who were running the show.

Peter, Darin, and Dede with Dr. John Polley
Photo Credit – Chris Clark, Spectrum Health Beat, 2017

Dr. Polley had planned out the entire surgery virtually. Every step of the process was documented, as well as when it would be done and who would do it. He showed us a thick playbook they would use in the operating room. I knew I was a complex case, so it was reassuring to see this much thought and attention to detail.

Following the appointments, we met up with Grandma who drove in from Indiana. She wanted to be there for my surgery and to help Mom and Dad during the first few days post-op. A representative from TMJ Concepts was also in town the night before. He had flown in from California, so we all went out to dinner together.

Mom couldn't resist asking if the TMJ rep would text her updates from the operating room. He agreed as long as my surgeons gave permission. It was going to be a long day with surgery anticipated to take over eight hours, so Mom liked the idea of being able to text someone in the OR.

The morning of surgery in pre-op was INTENSE. Imagine sixteen years of build up to this one surgery that had taken over a year to plan. The fear and relief were overwhelming. I tried to comprehend how much my face was going to change, but it was nearly impossible to imagine.

We always request two things before surgery: a Child Life Specialist and anti-anxiety medication. I like to say this is best for everyone involved. After years of surgeries, I have overwhelming anxiety in pre-op. My biggest fear is needles, especially the I.V. Something about it totally freaks me out.

Child Life Specialists are the angels of pediatric hospitals. They know how to help you cope with stress and fear, and they explain things in ways kids and teens understand. They understand that medical PTSD is a very real condition, and they have always been a source of comfort and support for me.

To be completely honest, anti-anxiety medication helps a lot too! I do okay initially in pre-op, but the anxiety becomes too overwhelming as activity picks up. The medication, or "goofy juice," as I like to call it, helps with the fear. It also provides some humorous entertainment.

Mom warns me not to post anything on social media, but I usually take off my hearing aid and claim not to hear her! We have some entertaining pre-op videos that I have no recollection of making, and I've sent texts that I don't remember typing. One time I snuck my phone into the operating room and took a pic of the ceiling before going under. Mom found it on my phone when the nurse brought it out to her!

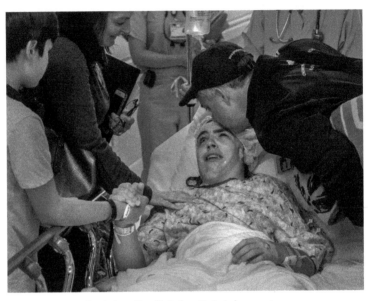

Dankelson Family before Peter's jaw surgery
Photo Credit – Chris Clark, Spectrum Health Beat, 2017

This surgery had so much emotional build-up that even the goofy juice didn't ease my fear. My anxiety went through the roof when I saw the stampede of feet behind the pre-op curtain. I knew that meant it was time for my ride to the OR, or as us frequent fliers call it, "wheels up."

I think everyone with me in pre-op kind of lost it at that point. I wanted one last look at my face, knowing it would never be the same again. I gave hugs to my grandma and parents. Jacob was last, and he didn't let go. He held my hand all the way down the hallway until he couldn't go any further.

Jacob was twelve for this surgery, and it was the first time he was old enough to fully comprehend what was going on. Jacob had also been hearing about this surgery for the past year, and he knew how anxious everyone was. He was worried about me too.

Siblings carry a lot of worry in families like ours. Mom and Dad knew how worried Jacob was because he didn't leave the lobby for the entire eight plus hours I was in surgery. Not even to get food! He was quiet and slept with my AC/DC blanket in the lobby.

As a distraction, Mom and Dad asked him to set up the new Nintendo Switch they'd purchased with gift money from family and friends. It gave him something helpful to do for me, and Mario Kart was a good way to pass the time.

Each specialist updated my family when their role in the playbook was done. Neurosurgery was one of the first finished. Their job was to cut the bone graft from my skull and replace it with titanium mesh. ENT was involved through most of the first half ensuring that my airway was secure, and no facial nerves were cut or damaged. My craniofacial surgeons, anesthesia, and all the support staff were there for the duration.

Once my family knew I was in recovery, they were told I would be moved immediately to the pediatric intensive care unit (PICU). That had been the plan all along, but, unfortunately, the PICU was full. I was instead put on a step-down floor. This meant I did not have as much nursing care and attention.

Once I was out of surgery, Dad and Jacob went back to our hotel to grab a few things. Mom and Grandma waited for me to be assigned a room. They were the first to see me.

After the shock of my swollen and bloodied face, Mom was in awe of my new profile. She said the jaw reconstruction gave me a "man chin." I looked significantly older, and it took Mom by surprise.

She had not anticipated feeling a sense of loss from missing my old face. Grieving my old face and voice (yes, my voice changed too), was something she had to work through once I was past the urgency of post-op care and recovery.

I was not fully conscious when Mom and Grandma saw me for the first time. I had a trach back in and was on a ventilator. My swollen jaw was wired shut, and I had stitches all over my head and face. I was also very pale from being in surgery so long.

Mom texted Dad my room number, but neither of them had thought to prepare Jacob for how I would look. He was scared the first time he saw me, and Mom and Dad assured him I would be okay.

Dad helped Jacob understand what each piece of equipment was doing, and they all took turns standing by the bed and holding my hand. They weren't sure how conscious I was, but they wanted me to know they were there. Mom whispered in my ear that I was out of surgery and that everything went very well.

Mom stayed with me that first night and encouraged Dad to do something fun with Jacob. The Grand Rapids Griffins hockey team was playing for the American Hockey League (AHL) Calder Cup that night. They went to the game and

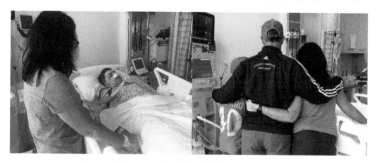

Peter with family after his eight hour jaw surgery
Photo Credit - Sharon Brockhaus, 2017

had a great time watching the Griffins win the cup. I know Jacob felt guilty having fun, but I'm glad they went. Grandma and Mom had dinner in my room and then Grandma went to her hotel and got some sleep.

I was sedated and on a ventilator that first night, so it was relatively quiet. I also had a large tube down my nose to vent air from my stomach. Nausea was a big concern because my mouth was wired shut. It was one of Mom's biggest fears for the two weeks I was wired. She was in constant fear of me aspirating from throwing up, which is why she carried wire cutters everywhere.

The first thing I remember when waking up was feeling like I had lost a boxing match. My face was swollen, and I could not move my mouth. I had a trach tube back in my neck that was attached to a ventilator. The inside of my mouth was dry and felt disgusting, and the large tube in my nose was unexpected and uncomfortable.

Mom was at my bedside as soon as I started waking up. I could not talk, so she tried to anticipate what questions I might have. She told me again that the surgery was over and that everything went well. She did her best to describe everything that was hooked up to me and why.

I was too groggy to type on my phone or write, so I used my hands and eyes to communicate. Mom was not good at guessing! I kept holding up two fingers, so she assumed I meant two of something. "Yes," she said, "You have two I.V.s." I would shake my head no.

She was still trying to guess what I was trying to say when Dad and Jacob arrived. They were glad to see that I was awake and tried to help Mom figure out what I wanted. I finally did the sign for the number two followed by making a zero shape with my hand. Dad said, "twenty?" Yes! I gave him a thumbs up and then pointed at the two of them.

Dad looked at Mom and said, "He is wishing us a happy twentieth anniversary." The day after my surgery was June 14, 2017. It was their twentieth wedding anniversary. FINALLY, they had figured it out! That had just about wiped me out trying to have them guess.

I felt bad that they were spending their big anniversary in the hospital, but that was the furthest thing from their mind. Mom and Dad planned to celebrate later when this was all behind us. None of us realized how long that would be.

Mom was still upset that I was not in the PICU. It was obvious there were too many patients and not enough staff. The floor doctors did not round on me until afternoon, and we were all trying to keep Mom from exploding by then.

She understood that I was stable and there were more urgent needs, but she also felt the hospital was not adequately staffed. The main thing I wanted was to be taken off the ventilator and to have the gigantic tube taken out of my nose. None of that could happen until rounds were done.

Things picked up in the afternoon once orders were given to the respiratory therapists. They took me off the ventilator and removed the trach. Dr. Polley came to check on me, and he pulled the very long tube out of my nose. He wasn't kidding that it went all the way down to my stomach. Wow!

Mom told my Dad and brother to sit down when he did it, which is a good thing because they both nearly passed out. I was even shocked at how long it was. It was like a magician pulling an endless number of scarves out of his sleeve. No wonder it was so uncomfortable!

The best thing that happened that day was when music therapy delivered an electric guitar to my room. I was able to hold it in my lap and feel the calming power of those strings. They invited me to visit the music room when I was able to get out of bed. That gave me something to work for.

Dad stayed with me the second night, but it was anything but quiet. His loud snoring coupled with the hospital beeps and alarms going off were too much. I didn't get any sleep with that obnoxious symphony. He was fired!

The second day post-op was when I started asking about discharge. I always like to know what I've got to do to earn my "get out of jail" card. If your vitals are good and pain is manageable, you can usually be discharged once you show that you can keep down food and get to and from the bathroom.

My first big move was from the bed to a chair. The second was transitioning off the I.V. for fluid and nutrition. I rarely used the feeding tube anymore, but I kept it knowing this surgery was coming. It was much easier to stay hydrated and

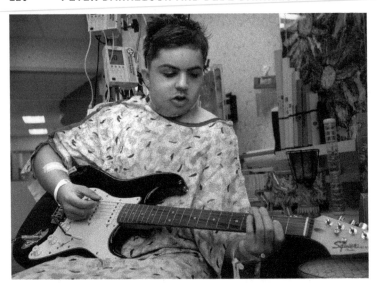

Peter in the music therapy room at Helen DeVos Children's Hospital
Photo Credit – Chris Clark, Spectrum Health Beat, 2017

get calories through the feeding tube since my jaw was wired shut.

Mom and Dad were out of practice doing tube feeding, but it came back to them quickly. Mom was anxious about feeding me too much, too fast. She was worried I would throw up and need to have the wires in my mouth cut. Dad and I let her stress about that. I promised to tell her if I felt full or uncomfortable at any time, and we started with small amounts.

I took my first field trip two days after the surgery. I'm sure you will not be surprised when I tell you it was to the music therapy room. I was looking and feeling rough, but there is no better medicine than plugging a guitar into an amp!

Mom was back on duty for night three. It was hell, even without Dad's snoring. Swelling and gunk trapped in your airway starts loosening up about forty-eight hours after surgery. That is one of the reasons you need to start moving as soon as safely possible. All that drainage sitting in your airway needs to be shaken loose and get out. Otherwise, you will end up with an infection in your lungs (pneumonia).

Everything started dislodging that third night, and it was scary. I struggled to clear my airway and breathe. I could not swallow, and there were times when I felt like I was drowning in my own saliva. I needed my mouth and trach stoma (hole in my neck) constantly suctioned. It literally sucked! No one got any rest that night.

We spent most of the fourth day taking short naps in between tube feedings. We took another field trip, this time to the Child Life room. Jacob and Dad enjoyed a game of air hockey, and I played video games. It was exhausting. I was shocked at how much effort it took to do anything.

Dr. Polley said this surgery was a marathon recovery and that my body needed a lot of rest and nutrition to recover. He wanted me home as soon as safely possible so that I could start to really heal. I was discharged five days after surgery, but it seemed like an eternity.

Dad and Jacob left the night before my discharge. We were four hours from home, and they decided to get a jump start to make sure everything was ready for my homecoming. Mom and I would follow the next day.

Before leaving, they sent Mom to the cafeteria. They wanted her to grab dinner and snacks because Dad knew she wouldn't leave me alone. On her elevator ride to the cafeteria, Mom ran into players from the Grand Rapids Griffins.

The city had a parade that day celebrating their championship win, and the players had the Calder Cup at the hospital. Mom, not one to miss an opportunity, asked if they could stop by my room. She explained that Jacob played hockey and was at the final game.

Mom was excited to do something fun for Jacob. He was surprised when the players showed up in my room with the cup and auto-

Jacob holding the AHL Calder Cup
Photo Credit - Dede Dankelson, 2017

graphed his shirt from the game. That visit was a good way to celebrate my discharge, and it was a well-earned reward for Jacob.

The three things I always miss when having surgery are my own bed, my dogs, and my guitars. More than anything I was looking forward to sleeping in my own bed. Mom was not so sure though.

I had my mouth wired shut and was coughing a lot. She was worried I was developing an upper-respiratory infection, and she didn't think it was safe for me to sleep alone. I was not happy about this development, but I also knew I wasn't going to win this argument.

Mom and Dad wanted me to sleep with my head elevated. They have an adjustable mattress that can be raised, so that was the best option. The next discussion was who would sleep in the room with me.

I had to choose between snoring Dad or Mom. Yeah, just what every sixteen-year-old boy wants! I went with Mom so that I could sleep, and she promised to stay as far on the other side of the mattress as she could.

The coughing and choking at night was excruciating, so I was kind of relieved that Mom was close. Seriously though, don't tell her I said that! The dogs sleep wherever Mom is, so they were happy to be my nurses too.

I knew the recovery after jaw reconstruction was going to be long and challenging, but I don't think any of us realized just how hard it was going to be. The first two weeks post-op were the worst because my mouth was tightly wired shut. I could not even sip water through a straw.

The feeding tube made it easier to consume enough calories for my body to heal, but it did not help the disgusting way my mouth felt. My tongue was dry, and I had stitches everywhere. With some practice, I figured out a way to squeeze water in my cheek and get it to the back of my throat. I was able to get small sips on my tongue that way, but it also resulted in a decent amount of choking.

Mom had a checklist of things that had to be done several times a day. I had to rinse and clean my mouth, do oral exercises, put ointment on the incision sites, and sit for tube feedings. Added to all that was breathing treatments because I did end up with a respiratory infection.

Mom had me in the pediatrician's office just two days after discharge. She couldn't handle another night listening to me cough and choke, and she was definitely at her breaking point.

I know this because she started crying in the doctor's office. The doctor and I were calming her down. I kept typing on my phone, "Mom, I'm fine. I'm going to be okay."

My refuge during recovery was my music room. Some days I did not have the energy to play but just being with my guitars was good therapy. It helped me stay positive and motivated me to recover. It also got me away from Mom but only if I took a bell with me. She had me carry one everywhere in case I needed help quickly.

After my respiratory infection cleared up, I talked Mom into letting me sleep alone. I still had about a week left with my jaw wired shut, but she knew I missed my room. We negotiated an agreement that I could sleep alone if I had the bell and my phone with me. All our bedrooms were on the same floor, so everyone was within "bell-hearing distance" even with the doors closed.

We all went to bed, and I was relishing my independence. Unfortunately, I knocked over the bell when I reached for my water bottle. You guessed it, Mom and the dogs came sprinting out of her bedroom quickly followed by Jacob. I couldn't say anything, but I held up the water bottle showing them what happened.

Where was Dad during this midnight chaos? Gleefully sound asleep in his own bed for the first time in weeks and snoring loudly. Mom was annoyed he didn't wake up, so she gave him a little love tap (more like a kick) when she went back to bed!

Two-weeks after surgery, I was back at Helen DeVos Children's Hospital for Dr. Polley to cut my wires. I was shocked at how stiff and foreign my jaw felt after the wires were cut. I had a completely different mouth, and it felt like a rusty hinge.

Dr. Polley showed me daily exercises to do, which was basically holding my mouth open as wide as I could for several seconds. Everything was in a different place too. I was not familiar with having so much room in my mouth, and I still had a splint covering my top teeth and palate (roof of my mouth).

The most frustrating part of the recovery was the constant drooling. Several parts of my face, especially around my lips were numb. I could not feel anything, and I was re-learning how to swallow. A dish towel to wipe my mouth went everywhere with me. It was so embarrassing!

Fortunately, I was headed into a crowd of people who understood exactly what I was going through. Our family attends an annual retreat at the end of every June. It is hosted by Children's Craniofacial Association, and it is a yearly high-

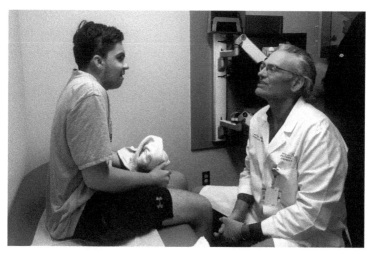

Peter and Dr. Polley after his jaw wires were cut
Photo Credit - Dede Dankelson, 2017

light for all of us. CCA families form an instant bond of understanding.

Kids and adults with craniofacial conditions meet others who look like they do and who have endured similar surgeries and social situations. Parents and siblings form friendships as well. We think of CCA as our tribe.

We did not know if I would feel good enough to make the retreat since it was only a few weeks after the jaw surgery. We all desperately needed to be with our tribe though, especially Mom. We were fortunate that the 2017 retreat was within driving distance.

The event was in Alexandria, Virginia, a suburb of Washington D.C., so we made a road trip out of it. The first leg was Illinois to Michigan for my doctor's appointment. The second leg was Michigan to Ohio, where we stayed overnight with my Dankelson grandparents. The final leg was Ohio to Virginia where we enjoyed three glorious days with CCA families.

Peter at the CCA Talent Show
Photo Credit - Dede Dankelson, 2017

I was still swollen and drooling, but at least my jaw was not wired shut anymore. CCA hosts a talent show every year, and I wanted to play guitar. The only time I had performed was at my high school talent show, and I was excited about having an audience again.

I had to wear a dish towel around my neck to catch the

drool while I played, but I did it. We jokingly called it "Rock and Drool" instead of "Rock and Roll." My best buddies, Chase and Jeremy, along with all the CCA families, cheered me on. I played an AC/DC cover of "Baby Please Don't Go." The entire ballroom was rocking!

I'm grateful that I made it to that retreat. It was a huge dose of support that we all needed, but it was also my last chance to hang out with Chase. The two of us met at our first retreat when I was four and he was five. Chase hadn't been to a retreat for several years, so it was fun to reconnect as teenagers.

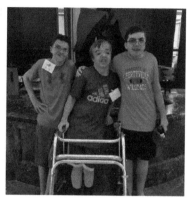

Jeremy, Chase, and Peter
Photo Credit - Dede Dankelson, 2017

Jeremy, Chase, and I loved attending activities together. Chase and I shared a love of music, and he played piano at the talent show. Sadly, Chase passed away just six months after the 2017 retreat. He had an undiagnosed craniofacial syndrome and was having seizures. He was a good friend, and I will always have fond memories of our time together.

The retreat gave us all a boost of strength, but the drudgery of recovery continued once we returned home. I still couldn't feel parts of my face or lips and swallowing and speech remained a struggle. Mom was getting frustrated with the tube feedings and wanted me to work harder to use a straw.

Six weeks after surgery I finally got the splint covering my top teeth and palate removed. My orthodontist was able to remove it, so we did not have to make another trip back to Michigan. That was pure bliss getting rid of that thing. We were all hoping I would be able to swallow easier with it out.

That July was a long month in our house. Jacob was invited to spend a week at the lake with friends, and Mom was relieved he was doing something fun. I was still exhausted all the time. This recovery felt like my body was running a marathon every day.

Mom was desperate to get out of the house and do something fun. She saw that Queen and Adam Lambert were coming to Chicago. She bought tickets for us to go while Jacob was at the lake, and I spent the week excited to see Brian May. He is truly one of my guitar heroes.

Peter at the United Center
Photo Credit - Dede Dankelson, 2017

Dad refused to go to the concert with me carrying a drool rag, so Mom wrapped a handkerchief around my wrist. She told me to wipe my mouth with that instead. We all agreed it was a much cooler look!

That concert was unbelievable. We didn't have the best seats, but it was so fun to feel the energy. Queen has such an incredible catalog of songs, and Adam Lambert's performance was on the mark. He did not try to replace Freddy. His performance complimented and honored him.

Back to the reality of home, Mom was at her wits end with the tube feedings. Dad also felt I needed to try harder. He bought Mom a plane ticket and sent her to see a friend for the weekend, promising that when she returned, I would be drinking through a straw.

Dad pushed me all weekend and came through on the promise. When Mom arrived home, I was drinking through a straw. I was also coughing and choking a lot. She looked at Dad and said, "You know he's aspirating, right?"

Dad said, "Yes, but he is drinking through a straw. He'll figure it out eventually." Mom was worried, but let it go, and I eventually stopped aspirating. Fortunately, it was before I developed another upper respiratory infection. I think they've been through enough challenges with me to know when to trust the other's strategy. I get the benefit of having them both support me in different ways. I don't always recognize their strategies as beneficial at the time, but I usually grow to appreciate them in retrospect.

The best thing that happened in July was the opening of School of Rock Libertyville, just a few miles from my house. I had been playing on my own for about a year and a half and was learning everything from *YouTube* videos. Mom and Dad wanted me to give lessons a try.

I was still drooling and embarrassed to go to the open house, but I enjoyed being at the school. As a kickoff for their opening, the school was having a one-week camp called *Metal Madness*. I was intimidated about playing with other students, but also very interested. Mom hoped it would give me a fun distraction.

That week at camp was my first experience playing in a

band. I really enjoyed it and met other kids who liked the same music. After that week I agreed to give lessons a try.

I was one of the founding students in School of Rock Libertyville's first performance group. That's a group that rehearses for several months and then plays at a local venue. Performing was my favorite part of being a School of Rock student.

Every three to four months, I got to choose from two to four themed offerings. I had weekly guitar lessons and band rehearsals that resulted in a local performance. The opportunity to perform for a live audience took my energy and enthusiasm to an entirely new level.

I was not excited about it in the beginning though, and I almost quit. I was used to choosing what songs I wanted to learn and practice. Being in a band means you work together, and everyone makes compromises on the song selection.

The first performance group offered at my School of Rock was The Beatles. Although I can now appreciate why they started with The Beatles, I was not a fan at the time. I didn't like the songs and wouldn't practice them.

Mom told me I was going to perform whether I learned the songs or not. She said, "You can learn the songs and have fun at the performance, or you can choose not to learn the songs and sound terrible. Either way, you're getting up on that stage." Dad was in full agreement.

I procrastinated until the week of the performance and then rushed to learn everything. I did not know the songs as well as I should've, but I did get on the stage. That's when I fell in love with performing.

I was much more excited about the second session because

it was a Zeppelin Tribute. I practiced a lot and was psyched for the performance. That Zeppelin show might still be my favorite performance group. We got to perform at a concert venue that had lights and full effects.

Being in the performance groups led to a spot in the House Band. That was when I really learned about working as a team! We had a bit of drama in the beginning, but those of us who stuck it out ended up having a great time and playing some awesome gigs like Summerfest in Milwaukee. I made a lot of great friends through School of Rock. Rehearsing and playing gigs with the House Band is where I spent most of my time the last two years of high school. We all shared a love for performing and being in a band.

Speaking of school, I started my junior year just two months after jaw surgery. What a first day back-to-school that was! No one could understand my speech, I was still worried about drooling, and people were surprised at how much my face changed. I was also exhausted just being at school for a full day.

I like to joke that my face changed every year of high school, and you can see it in the yearbook photos. My face was still swollen for school pictures when junior year began, and I had to put up with that photo on my student ID all through senior year too.

Being back at school was tiring, but it was also mentally good for me. I hadn't seen any school friends since the surgery, so I had a lonely summer. Seeing everyone at school lifted my mood and getting back into a routine felt good.

I continued to heal and recover as school got underway. Junior year was busy, but I always found time to practice gui-

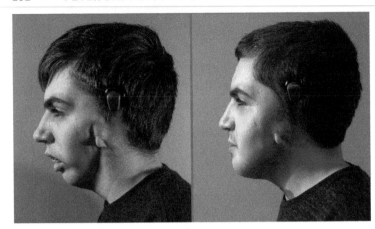

Peter before (June 2017) and after (August 2017) jaw surgery
Photo Credit – Chris Clark, Spectrum Health Beat, 2017

tar. I spent a few nights every week at School of Rock, and the House Band often had gigs on the weekends.

Excitement for the *Wonder* movie was also heating up. CCA Families were invited to attend the movie premiere in Beverly Hills. That was a fun night experiencing the lights and glamour, watching the movie, and attending the after party. I snagged a selfie with Owen Wilson and reconnected with the younger actors I'd met on the movie set.

Peter at the Wonder movie premiere
Photo Credit - Dede Dankelson, 2017

The movie's release brought in more speaking requests. Mom and I visited schools in Illinois one to two times a week. We also traveled to Michigan to speak at a medical conference and tied in a few school visits there. It was fun being back in my home state and staying with friends.

During the Q & A at one of the schools, a student asked me if I had any mentors. Since we were back in Michigan, I told the story about how Coach Babcock invited me to a couple Detroit Red Wings games when I was younger. I said, "Coach told me to be a difference maker, and look what I'm doing now. I'm talking to your school about why it's important to be kind."

One of the teachers from that school was friends with Mike Babcock's daughter. She shared what I'd said, and it reached Coach. Babcock was no longer with the Red Wings but head coach for the Toronto Maple Leafs. His public relations manager reached out to us via email.

Mom was surprised to receive the message having not been aware of all the behind-the-scenes communication. Coach said he'd like to meet me again, so Mom and Dad planned a surprise trip to Toronto during my holiday break.

I had no idea where we were going, but Jacob saw Mom grab our passports. We were guessing all the way to the airport until we checked in and saw our flight was headed to Toronto. That's when Mom and Dad told us we'd be going to a game and meeting Coach Babcock again.

We had a great family trip to Toronto visiting the Hockey Hall of Fame and exploring the city. Coach invited us to watch a practice, and then we got a tour of the locker room. The entrance to the player area has a big sign that reads, "Honor, Pride, Courage." I love that.

Dankelson Family in Toronto with Coach Mike Babcock
Photo Credit – Steve Keogh, Toronto Maple Leafs, 2018

We sat down with Coach and talked about how his advice to "be a difference maker" became our family mantra. He asked about the school assemblies and said he was proud of what we were doing. It was great to reconnect, and this time Jacob got to meet Coach too. Jacob's the hockey player in our family, so this was exciting for him. We all laughed when Coach looked at Jacob and said, "Are you any good?"

Toronto played Detroit that weekend, which is one of the reasons Mom and Dad picked that game. We're loyal Detroit Red Wings fans. I felt bad cheering against coach's team, but he understood. It was an exciting game that went into over-time. Detroit lost five to four, so Coach got that one.

Meeting Coach again reignited Mom's passion to continue making a difference in schools. She periodically asked me if I wanted to continue doing it, and I always said, "Yes." I enjoyed speaking with students and feeling the positive energy from assemblies as much as she did.

The second half of my junior year went by quickly. With the jaw surgery behind us, there were no major medical issues taking up space in my head. I didn't carry that constant anxiety with me every day. I wanted to have the hole in my neck closed, but I also wanted a break from it all. We all did.

It was around this time that Mom began thinking about plans for after I finished high school. Even with a college degree, people with a facial difference struggle to live independent lives. Anti-discrimination laws have helped with hiring, but the social stigma remains. We have pre-existing conditions and extensive medical needs as well as speech, hearing, and learning disabilities that are obstacles to employment.

Through our involvement with Children's Craniofacial Association, my family knows many adults living with craniofacial syndromes. My parents heard their struggles and stories and were concerned about my future as well.

I was unsure about going to college, but I knew I wanted to keep playing guitar. Choosing a music career is not an easy or traditional path, but it parallels my life. I didn't have a traditional childhood, so doing something non-traditional after high school didn't seem that crazy. School and academics were always challenging for me, and college didn't feel like the next step.

I considered music programs, but I've never learned to read music. I don't aspire to teach, and I prefer to study other artists and learn on my own. Mom and Dad wanted to give me the space and time to explore and be creative, but they also wanted me to become financially independent.

With Dad's support, Mom established a limited liability company (LLC) for our motivational speaking business. She felt it was the right time to begin charging a fee for our school visits. This could bring in revenue while I pursued my dream of becoming a musician.

When thinking about what to call the company, Mom went back to where our story started. The NICU updates she wrote after I was born had been referred to as "Pete's Diary." That's the name she used for the LLC and our new website.

Now set up with our own identity, Mom began to lessen our association with *Wonder*. She felt the #ChooseKind message was becoming diluted into simply "be nice." Kindness is not as passive. Being kind means you have the courage to stand up for others. Confident kids can do that. They don't succumb as easily to peer pressure.

Sharing my story in a way that encouraged self-acceptance became our new focus. I talked about how empowering it is to embrace what makes you different, how you build mental grit by choosing courage over fear, and how you attract genuine friendships by being yourself.

Students saw that I lived confidently with a facial difference, remained positive after so many surgeries, and found joy playing guitar. They saw that I made supportive friendships through Children's Craniofacial Association and School of Rock. They were impressed with how I bravely shared my story with large audiences around the country. If I could do all that, they could do hard things too.

As my junior year drew to a close, Mom decided it was time to learn if we could get the hole in my neck closed. She knew I would need sleep studies and exploratory scopes to find out if my airway was enlarged enough from the jaw

Peter before (2016) and after (2019) jaw surgery with trach stoma still open
Photo Credit - Dede Dankelson & Images by Marie Moore, 2017

surgery. Appointments were made, and we embarked on the ultimate goal of closing my open trach stoma.

I've had a sleep study nearly every year since birth, and I call them "no-sleep studies." Mom has never been to one. She says it is a perfect guys' night for me and Dad to bond. I'd say that's a reach, but neither of us are willing to argue with her about it.

If you've never had a sleep study, Google it. You'll find photos that show how many sensors they stick all over your head and body. It's a lot! That, combined with the thought of someone watching you sleep all night in a strange place, makes for a restless night.

When I was little and scared of the equipment, it was a wrestling match to get everything on. Now I know it's nothing to fear. Well, except for when they pull those stickers off my hairy legs! It also takes a few washings to get all the glue out of my hair.

Dad and I had our guys' night out at the sleep lab, and

it was a typical no-sleep night for me. I'm not sure what was worse... the sensors, equipment noises, or Dad's snoring. As we waited for results, I became excited about the idea that my trach stoma might actually be closed. I'd been waiting my entire life for this to happen.

Unfortunately, the sleep study did not show promising results. I was still having obstructive sleep apnea when lying down. The question was why? What was causing it now that my airway was larger? Doctors were perplexed, and I was frustrated.

We consulted with two airway specialists who recommended further testing to solve the mystery. This involved a couple more trips to the operating room for scopes of my upper airway, a botched MRI scan that still gives me nightmares, and another year of trying to figure out what to do.

All those tests finally revealed that an area at the base of my tongue was collapsing against my larynx (voice box) when I laid down. This collapse was obstructing my breathing when sleeping. The ENT who discovered this said there was nothing more that could be done surgically. My new "man chin" was awesome, but not enough to reach my dream of closing the trach stoma.

I was referred to a pulmonary specialist about trying a CPAP machine. CPAP stands for continuous positive airway pressure. The pressurized air from a CPAP machine opens your airway when sleeping. Doctors thought this might resolve my obstruction.

With no more surgical options, the CPAP was our last resort. This was where my medical journey stood as I started senior year of high school. Mom always had a goal of getting the trach stoma closed before I graduated. Her deadline was closing in quickly!

Because of my age, we consulted with an adult, instead of a pediatric, provider. This was quite a startling transition after spending my life in pediatric waiting rooms. Mom and I went from waiting in lobbies full of active toddlers and Disney movies to elderly folks with walkers and oxygen carts. Talk about culture shock!

The appointment went well, and we both liked the pulmonologist (lung doctor). He reviewed my latest sleep study and agreed that a CPAP might be the answer. He knew I wasn't thrilled about wearing the mask at night, so we looked at a few options. The least bulky mask was a nasal cannula that didn't' cover my entire face. I agreed to give it a try, not realizing that I've never breathed through my nose when sleeping.

To see if the CPAP would help me, we first had to find a way to seal the trach hole. If it wasn't plugged, air would just escape through the stoma (hole in my neck). The challenge was finding a bandage and adhesive that was strong enough to keep my airway sealed but not so harsh that it irritated my skin. Any skin breakdown around the trach hole would be a party place for infections.

Every time I exhaled, air took the path of least resistance and pushed up against the bandage. If I sneezed or coughed, I'd blow the entire thing off. There's a good reason why CPAP doesn't work if you have a trach. It's like trying to inflate a leaky tire!

The first night was a total disaster. We managed to seal up the hole, but we didn't realize that I'm a mouth breather when sleeping. The nasal cannula kept me awake all night.

Every time I fell asleep, the air pressure through my nose would wake me up. At some point I threw it across the room!

I obviously needed a full-face mask. The second mask I tried was a winner. It was comfortable and covered both my nose and mouth. The only remaining problem was keeping the bandage sealed, which was an ongoing challenge.

It took several months to acquire enough data and confirm that I was breathing well with the CPAP. Mom spent a lot of that time fighting with our insurance company. They argued I was not using the equipment consistently and, therefore, did not need the equipment. Wrong!

I could not use the machine for more than one to two consecutive nights. I would either cough and break the bandage seal or my skin would become irritated from the harshness of the adhesive, requiring me to take a break from using it. The last thing I wanted was an infection from skin breakdown.

I eventually clocked enough hours per night within a thirty-day period to appease the insurance company and lower Mom's blood pressure. Despite the struggle with insurance, I was excited to learn that the CPAP appeared to be working. I was not obstructing while sleeping with it on, and the pulmonary doctor was more than satisfied with my results.

He gave me his approval to have the tracheostomy hole closed. Wait a minute, what?! I was in disbelief after waiting eighteen years to hear a doctor say that! I started letting myself dream about swimming and going tubing. Oh, and kayaking—all the things I could never safely do.

Mom set up appointments to consult with specialists once again. We had never gotten this far into my airway closure, and we did not anticipate it would be a complex or complicated surgery. At the most, Mom thought I might need a skin graft to cover the hole.

After eighteen years of experience, you would think we would know better than to make such assumptions. Mom and I left the first consult in a state of shock. This ENT's opinion was that my airway could not be closed on the outside without reinforcing it on the inside.

He said I needed cartilage grafted around my trachea to ensure it would not collapse internally. This is a delicate surgery called laryngotracheal reconstruction or LTR. Recovery includes being intubated with a tube down your nose for seven to ten days to secure your airway while the trachea graft heals.

My appointment was first thing in the morning, and I was planning to go directly from the doctor's office to school. Mom and I drove in stunned silence for a few minutes before she asked if I felt up to being at school. When she looked over at me, I was starting to break down, and I said, "I can taste anesthesia in my mouth right now." As I've said, medical PTSD is very real.

The drive to school was not long. When we got there, Mom sat in the parking lot with me. She said I did not have to go to school, but we both knew it would be a good distraction vs sitting at home full of anxiety. She reminded me there was no deadline or urgency to have this surgery, that we would get other opinions, and that I would make the final decision.

The most important thing to know about medicine is that it is called a practice for a reason. There are no absolute right answers, and doctors frequently have different opinions on how to achieve the same result.

When I had my first reconstructive surgeries as a toddler,

Mom and Dad had four different opinions from four well-respected craniofacial surgeons. They each had their own recommendation for what surgeries I needed, at what age, and in what order. Mom and Dad had to take in all the opinions, do their own research, and choose what doctor and approach felt right.

One thing I've learned from my parents is to always get a second or even third opinion. Find two to three surgeons who are highly qualified and skilled at whatever you are considering. Meet them in person if possible and do not be afraid to ask questions.

Because I was older and able to make my own healthcare decisions, Mom and Dad felt their job was to get answers to my questions and to ask questions I might not think about. They would get as many opinions as I needed. There was no rush, and I had to be confident in whatever decision I made.

The second opinion was completely different. This surgeon did not feel I needed the internal graft. His approach was to start simple and move to the more complex surgery only if necessary. He would first core the trach stoma, which is burning the skin around the trach hole to encourage new skin growth. This is done in hopes that the body heals itself. Kind of like how new skin covers a scab.

I was not confident that would happen since the size of my trach stoma was so large. It hadn't even shrunk a little bit in fourteen years. This process would take months of waiting to see if the stoma closed on its own. If it didn't work, I would have scar tissue making subsequent surgeries riskier. On the plus side, the surgery was quick and outpatient. It was certainly the least invasive approach.

I wanted the simple solution. I wanted the quicker, outpatient surgery. I also knew that it did not feel right. I was not comfortable with how unconcerned the second ENT was about something as important as my airway.

Mom suggested we request another consult with the first surgeon and share the second ENT's recommendation. This would give us an opportunity to ask the first surgeon why he did not recommend trying the least invasive approach first.

We discussed both approaches with the first surgeon and learned why he did not recommend trying the less invasive approach. He agreed it was a feasible option, but he also did not feel it would work. He was concerned that if the easier option failed, it would make the reconstructive surgery riskier.

I considered how I felt about both surgeons, their team, and the two different hospitals. When making such a major medical decision, you must be comfortable and confident with the surgeon and medical team you choose. If you do not have that level of confidence or something just does not feel right, you need to continue looking.

Deep down I knew what choice was best for me. It is not the one I wanted, but it was the best option for my long-term health. It was extremely disappointing because I thought my hardest surgeries were behind me. I needed time to reflect and mentally prepare myself before agreeing to have the bigger surgery.

Mom and I were booked to speak at schools in California, and we decided to wait on making a final decision until after the trip. It was our fourth consecutive year speaking to sixth graders in Capistrano Unified School District, representing

Children's Craniofacial Association and the #ChooseKind movement inspired by *Wonder*.

It was a busy week of one to two school assemblies per day, but we had a weekend set aside for fun. Mom decided it was the perfect time to distract us from thinking about the surgery. We had been to Los Angeles quite a bit the last few years, but I'd never been to Norman's Rare Guitars.

Mom didn't know anything about Norm's, but I watched all the "Guitar of the Day" videos with Mark Agnesi. It was a dream of mine to visit the store and stay on Sunset Blvd where so much rock & roll history happened.

Mom booked a hotel on the strip, made reservations at the Rainbow Room, and got us tickets to see an eighties cover band at the Whiskey a Go Go. She also took me to Norman's Rare Guitars. I swear it was like walking through the gates of heaven!

We got to the store right when it opened and were the first ones through the door. Mom struck up a conversation with Mark, who asked what we were in town for. That, of course, lead to a conversation about the school assemblies.

She told Mark I asked to visit the store several times on previous trips, but we never had time. She said the store visit was part of a fun weekend to distract us from all the medical stuff. While they talked, I browsed the inventory and played one guitar after another.

One of the guitars I picked up was a Stevie Ray Vaughan Stratocaster. I was loving it, and Norm's videographer, Jen Manalo, asked if she could record me playing it for their "Straturday" post. "Ummm, YEAH!"

While I continued playing guitars, Mom tried to stay out

of the way as the store got busier. After a while, Mark offered to show us some of the backroom inventory and rock memorabilia. I was in awe. Getting to stand where they film "Guitar of the Day" videos was so special.

Mom, having never watched the videos, had no clue how exciting it was. She could, however, appreciate a simple act of kindness. It really meant a lot to her that Mark did that for me. That's what we mean when we talk about the importance of kindness. This is a special memory for both of us.

Norm was also very gracious. He's a big supporter of antibullying, so he was interested in my story. He asked if I would record a second video talking about Goldenhar Syndrome and why kindness matters. It wasn't my best interview.

Peter with Mark Agnesi and the SRV Stratocaster at Norman's Rare Guitars
Photo Credit - Dede Dankelson and Jen Manalo, 2019

I was pretty star struck sitting on the famous couch with everyone in the store watching.

The visit to Norm's was the highlight of that trip for both of us. Seeing me so happy made Mom happy. So happy, in fact, that she bought the SRV Strat! I love the guitar, but it's the memory of that day that really makes it special. Thanks to the staff at Norman's Rare Guitars for welcoming us into your family.

We spent the rest of our time walking up and down Sunset. Lunch at The Rainbow Room was amazing with so much rock & roll history on the walls, and the eighties cover band at The Whiskey was fantastic. Nuno Bettencourt, from the band Extreme, made a surprise appearance during their set. It was a perfect way to wrap up the weekend.

In the morning we headed back to Orange County for a week of school assemblies. The positive energy from visiting the schools and interacting with students gave us both a break from the medical stress. When we returned home, it was time to decide about the surgery and when to schedule it.

This was early spring of my senior year, and I didn't want to miss prom or graduation. I had also auditioned to be a School of Rock AllStar and was waiting to find out if I had made it. AllStars are the best musicians from School of Rock's global network of franchises. Being eighteen and a new student, this was my first and only chance to audition.

Students selected by their local franchise are invited to submit a performance video to School of Rock's International AllStars Team. These judges watch the videos and invite selected students to a live audition. From there, the judges determine who makes the final AllStars Group.

I worked hard on my performance video and was invited to a live audition in April. We were all hoping I would make the AllStars and have this special opportunity to tour.

As a family, we decided that I would take a gap year and schedule the surgery for early fall. This meant I could finish high school without interruption and enjoy the summer. Mom and Dad preferred this because Jacob was starting high school, and they wanted to wait until after he was settled into a new routine.

With surgery put off, I fully enjoyed my senior year. I was part of the Homecoming and Turnabout Courts, invited to play the National Anthem before a basketball game, fully involved in Best Buddies and Young Life Clubs, and still speaking at schools about kindness and inclusion.

Another highlight from that year was being recognized as a "Patient of Courage" by the American Society of Plastic Surgeons. They produced a video about my jaw surgery and honored me and Dr. Girotto at their annual meeting in Chicago.

For spring break, Mom planned a family trip to Italy where we had tours of Rome, Florence, and Venice. I was finally able to visit St. Peter's Square at the Vatican. I'd always wanted to see it in person since the Papal Conclave during 2005. As we waited for a new Pope to be announced, the media kept showing coverage from St. Peter's Square. I was five and referred to it as "My Square."

I love history, so this trip was incredibly interesting to me. Jacob preferred the gelato and shopping to the tours, so there was something for him too. I even played guitar one night with a street musician.

On the train from Rome to Florence, Mom read about a

leather shop called Benheart in one of her travel books. She shared it with Dad because the story resonated with her. I've included it here, and I think you'll understand why Mom felt an instant connection:

Benheart is an extraordinary story about creativity and fulfilling a dream. Ben was born in Fes, Morocco, home to the oldest leather tannery in the world and was just a child when he arrived in Scandicci, Italy which is famous for its artisanal leather production. This is where he began to dream of creating his first leather jacket collection.

Tragedy struck ten years ago while Ben was playing football and was abruptly diagnosed with a life-threatening illness, finding himself in need of a new heart.

When all hope seemed lost, a miracle was granted via an organ donor and Ben received a second chance at life, which sparked a rebirth. He arose from his surgery with a purpose: to fulfill his dream to create artisanal luxury leather goods in the birth place of the Renaissance, Florence – a city known for craftsmanship from time immemorial: Leonardo...Michelangelo...Vasari... Gucci.

Ben was reborn, full of ambition and determination and is driven by the thought that he is not only fulfilling his dreams, but also those of his donor who was not granted a second chance.

The company embraces the name Benheart: the logo - a key with the upper portion shaped in a heart. The key that opened Ben's heart and will continue to open doors for all those associated with the brand. It symbolizes a story of love, altruism, friendship, and courage.

The story was somewhat forgotten once we arrived in Florence as we rushed to keep up with Mom's busy itinerary. Walking through the shopping district our first night, though, we walked by the store.

What a beautiful place. Designed to look and feel like an old Italian leather shop, the store is stunning. Mom and Dad had me try on a jacket and decided I should get one. The artisan who helped us was great and explained how they would tailor the jacket to fit me perfectly.

Ben happened to be in the store that evening and introduced himself. With help from translators, Mom shared how she read about his story, and Dad explained a little bit of mine to him. I showed Ben a few of my guitar videos, and he was impressed.

Peter with Hicham Benmbarek Sheraian (Ben) at Benheart in Florence, Italy
Photo Credit - Dede Dankelson, 2019

After ordering my jacket, Ben invited me and Jacob to select a belt and buckle that would also be customized to our measurements. How nice was that? I took a picture with Ben, and we left the store with plans to come back in a few days.

Dad knew Mom loved the shoes, so he wasn't surprised when she bought a pair when we returned. Benheart is a brand I'm proud to endorse, and I've stayed in touch with both Ben and the shop on social media.

My senior year wound down quickly after returning home. In May I received the news that I made the School of Rock 2019 AllStars Tour, so I was super excited about that.

Prom and graduation were a blast, but I was a little sad as school ended. I had grown to love the students and teachers at Libertyville High School. I knew I would miss seeing many of them every day.

Summer was shaping up to be a fun distraction from worrying about the airway surgery. It started with a trip to Boston where I was invited to represent Harmony 4 Hope in the "Battle of the Biotech Bands." It's a fun, but serious competition where employees from biotech companies form bands and compete for charity. Employees from Sanofi Genzyme selected Harmony 4 Hope as their charity. Their band was called Led Zymmelin.

I'm not kidding when I say this was a lit party! Over six hundred attendees filled the Royale Nightclub in Boston to watch four bands compete. These men and women are scientists and industry leaders who are also talented musicians. Led Zymmelin invited me to play "Walk This Way" by Aerosmith with them.

We didn't win, but the competition is set up to be a win-win for everyone. Half of the money raised goes to the winning band's charity and the remaining fifty percent is split equally between the other three. H4H used their donation to distribute grants supporting research studies for the treatment and cure of rare diseases.

Another great distraction that summer was a trip to Nashville. Mark Agnesi, who I met at Norman's Rare Guitars in Los Angeles, had taken a job with Gibson. He invited me to a private tour of the factory. We weren't going to pass up that opportunity, so we made a family road trip to Tennessee.

Watching how much detail goes into the making of each

guitar was incredible. Gibson employees are artisans, and every guitar is brought to life through their craftsmanship. Mark showed us each step in the process, and we also toured the Custom Shop. I enjoyed trying out all the models in the showroom and could've spent all day there.

We met Cesar Gueikian, President of Gibson Brands. Mark told him about the school assemblies I was doing, and he loved that we were championing kindness and antibullying. Neither of them liked that I was playing a Taylor acoustic at the schools though, so they gave me a new G45 acoustic. Wow!

Dede and Peter with Mark Agnesi at Gibson in Nashville
Photo Credit - Darin Dankelson, 2019

The model Cesar gave me is the one he approved for production, so it's extra special. The people we've met at Gibson, including those in the Los Angeles showroom, have all been incredibly kind. I'm grateful to have their continued support.

Nashville is a great city for a "Guitar Safari," so we also visited Carter's Vintage Guitars and Rumble Seat Music. Both owners interviewed me for their social media channels and promoted the Pete's Diary mission to amplify positive vibes.

After Nashville, I was immersed in practicing for the School of Rock AllStars tour and summer gigs with the Libertyville House Band. July and August went by quickly. I played stages in Chicago, Toronto, Detroit, Pittsburgh, and

Cleveland plus Summerfest in Milwaukee and Lollapalooza in Chicago. We had local gigs on the weekends, and I loved every minute because I knew it was ending soon.

With the fall I not only faced airway surgery, but also the loss of being a School of Rock student. At eighteen, I aged out and could no longer perform with the House Band. My social life was with School of Rock, and I would miss hanging out with those kids. Anxiety over the upcoming surgery began to consume most of my thoughts.

SIX

Using Music to Persevere

The first half of my gap year was busy with five surgeries between September – November of 2019. As my classmates headed off to college, I headed into the operating room at Ann & Robert H. Lurie Children's Hospital of Chicago.

One of the hardest things about the airway surgery was not knowing how long I would be in the hospital. We were told a minimum of two weeks and possibly up to four weeks. It was overwhelming to think of being in the hospital for a month.

The surgery was scheduled for early morning, so we spent the night in Chicago at a hotel near the hospital. Mom, Dad, and Grandma were with me. In pre-op I started thinking about how I'd had this hole in my neck for nineteen years and had never learned how to breathe without it. Would my body know what to do? It was nerve wracking to think about.

Faith in my family and trust in my surgeons comfort me the most before a surgery. I knew I was in good hands with Dr. Jonathan Ida and Lurie's Aerodigestive Team, and I was ready to get it over with. Living with the impending knowledge of surgery is mentally exhausting, and I'd had this one hanging over my head for six to nine months. I could sense my parents were extremely anxious about this one too.

The Laryngo Tracheal Reconstruction (LTR) was my thirty first surgery. It was six hours long with several steps involved. One of the unknowns was where the cartilage used to reinforce my trachea would come from.

Rib cartilage is routinely used for LTR procedures. Because of my age, Dr. Ida told us that he might be able to take cartilage from my thyroid instead. He wouldn't know, however, until I was in the operating room where he

Peter with trach stoma & feeding tube
Photo Credit - Images by Marie Moore, 2015

could look at the tissue. Taking cartilage from the thyroid would mean no incision in my chest, less pain, and a quicker recovery.

In planning appointments, Mom asked about having my feeding tube removed during this surgery hoping to get a two-for-one deal. Her primary goal since the NICU days was to have both the trach and feeding tube sites closed. After nineteen years, she still wasn't giving up.

Dr. Ida, however, wanted to use it by replacing the gastrostomy tube (g-tube) with a jejunostomy tube (j-tube). A j-tube bypasses the stomach and provides liquid nutrition into your intestine. Bypassing the stomach would prevent aspiration, acid reflux, or vomiting from going into my lungs. Any of those complications could jeopardize the trachea graft. It was an easy decision to do this since I already had the g-tube site.

Mom was promised the g-tube could be removed in a subsequent surgery. I would need several bronchoscopies (airway scopes) following the graft surgery. So, I guess the two-for-one deal was more of a benefit for the surgical team. Sorry Mom!

A peripherally inserted central catheter (PICC) line was inserted by the angioplasty team. A PICC line serves a similar purpose as an I.V., but it's longer and reaches the larger, central veins near your heart. This is typical if you need long-term I.V. medications. It reduces the need to remove and place a new I.V. multiple times, irritating your smaller veins. Because the PICC line is so close to your heart, it needs to be inserted by specialists and carefully monitored.

As with any surgery, there was good and bad news. The good news was surgeons were able to take cartilage for the graft from my thyroid instead of my rib. That meant less pain and quicker healing since I didn't have an incision in my chest.

The bad news was that they couldn't intubate me nasally. My facial bone structure and upper airway complications made it impossible to get the tube safely secured. Specialists had to insert the tube through my mouth instead. This was necessary to secure my airway while the trachea graft healed.

If I had been intubated through my nose, as planned, I could've been untethered from the ventilator. That's what we were expecting. Being intubated through my mouth meant I had to remain on the ventilator while the graft healed.

Having a big tube down the back of your throat is uncomfortable. I couldn't swallow and needed my mouth suctioned constantly. I couldn't move my head, and coughing was painful. Mom says this was the most excruciating thing she's had to sit through. This surgery scared her and Dad more than any I'd had before and watching me struggle on the ventilator was pure hell for them.

Many people who need to be on a ventilator are sedated for comfort, but Dr. Ida wanted to keep me partially awake if I could tolerate it. Long-term sedation requires a longer hospital stay because you need to be weaned off the narcotics.

I had some strong anti-anxiety and pain meds, but I was awake and communicating during the time I was on the ventilator. I have a spotty memory of those five days, which I'm grateful for. Mom and Dad were grateful for the one-to-one nursing care I had in Lurie's Pediatric Intensive Care Unit (PICU). Even with the extra monitoring, they would never leave me alone.

The first few days after surgery, Mom and Dad took turns sleeping in my room while the other stayed at Ronald McDonald House. I was so medicated that Dad's snoring didn't matter! Having a room at Ronald McDonald House gave them a place to sleep, shower, eat, and do laundry. Something as simple as taking a shower means a lot when you're stuck in the hospital 24/7.

My brother started his first year of high school just a few weeks before this surgery, so he couldn't be at the hospital with me. My surgery was on a Tuesday, and he didn't see me until Friday night.

I was so heavily sedated that I barely remember him visiting, but I do remember Jacob putting a guitar in my lap. I couldn't move my head, but I could run my fingers over the strings. The guitar was a gift from Jacob's hockey team at Carmel Catholic High School. All the players signed it, which made it extra special.

Jacob with the guitar signed by his hockey team
Photo Credit - Dede Dankelson, 2019

As with other surgeries, we did not get through this time alone. My Grandma was with us at the hospital, and we had the support of many friends helping us at home. Knowing Jacob was with friends helped Mom and Dad both logistically and emotionally.

Kindness comes in many forms, and every single act lifted us up. Mom was especially grateful for the Starbucks gift cards that kept her going! Our Pete's Diary social media followers were also a great source of support.

Fans on Twitter and Instagram started sending me Funko Pop figures. That's how my collection got started. The first one I received was, of course, Angus Young.

The Angus figure came to the hospital with me and even hung out in the operating room during surgery. Mom used it to post "Updates from Angus" where she would take a photo of him somewhere in my room and send out an update. It was an amusing distraction.

Grandma encouraged Mom and Dad to go out to dinner one night, but they weren't gone long. Emerging from the hospital amid exhaustion and worry is unsettling. You feel out of place, like you're on a strange planet. There is simply no relaxing when your child is in the hospital, no matter what their age.

Angus Young Funko Pop
Photo Credit - Dede Dankelson, 2019

After five difficult days and nights on the ventilator, it was time to go back into the operating room and see how the graft was healing. Mom and Dad anxiously awaited news. They prayed it would be good, and I could be taken off the vent.

I went directly from the OR back to my room in the PICU. Mom and Dad spoke there with Dr. Ida who informed them that everything was healing very nicely. He said that I could have the breathing tube removed once I was fully awake and alert.

I was still sedated as they talked. Mom and Dad were so excited to share the good news with me that they did their best to wake me up. Dad started playing AC/DC's Riff Raff on his phone, and he put it next to my ear. They knew I was conscious enough to hear when they saw my foot tapping under the blankets. Then I started playing air guitar with my hands!

The ICU nurse monitored my vitals as my parents coaxed me awake with AC/DC. What a great way to wake up from anesthesia! I highly recommend it. They turned down the music as I became more alert and shared the good news with me.

Once I understood what was about to happen, I shook myself awake even more. The nurse called for the respiratory team who would do the extubation. I'm glad I didn't have much time to think about how that would happen because I was still in shock over how long that tube was.

Watching respiratory pull that thing out reminded me of someone from the circus swallowing a long sword! Very freaky! It felt great to finally close my mouth and talk again though. My voice was hoarse, but I didn't care. It's amazing what you take for granted until it's taken away.

Peter seven days after surgery
Photo Credit - Dede Dankelson, 2019

Being intubated on less narcotics for fewer days meant that my recovery went much faster. Physical therapy helped me go for small walks on the floor and get moving again. I was weak, and my shoulder ached from lying in bed so long. It felt good to get out of that bed and turn my head from side to side.

Spending so much time in hospitals gives me a different perspective than most. As Mom and I took one of my first walks, I told her how lucky I am. She looked at me like I was kind of crazy for saying that. I did feel fortunate though.

Sure, being on the vent for several days and having surgery sucked, but I was otherwise healthy and would recover. The kid in the room next to me coded the night before. I don't know what his situation was, but it was a reminder that I wasn't battling the worst situation in that hospital.

Mom understood because she had seen a lot from our hospital stays. She remembers hearing parents ordering a wheelchair for their paralyzed son, learning of babies who became angels, and seeing children alone in the hospital because their parents needed to work.

You develop empathy from these experiences, and you also learn that life is all about the perspective you choose. There is always someone better off and there is always someone worse off. That doesn't lessen the pain of what you're going through, but it does remind you that everyone is fighting their own battle.

I was transferred out of ICU the day after I was free of the ventilator. Mom and I were thrilled to get a room with a window (like I said, it's the small things you take for granted!). Since I was out of critical care, Dad went back to work and handled things at home while Mom bunked at the hospital.

I had my Gibson acoustic with me, but I was itching to plug into an amp. The hospital had a few electric guitars, and the first field trip we took was to the music therapy room. I was there every chance I got and even played on Lurie's in-hospital TV station once.

Physical therapy was going great, so the next hurdle was getting the j-tube removed. I was desperate for a drink of water and some Gino's Pizza. Once Dr. Ida gave the all clear for eating, a team came to remove the j-tube and put my g-tube back in.

Gino's is on the same block as Lurie Children's Hospital

of Chicago, and Mom was more than happy to wait for the pizza. I suppose she earned some time out of the hospital room. We enjoyed that pizza in our room with a window view, and Mom recorded me playing my guitar after dinner.

Mom recognized the song I was playing by Jared James Nichols. I introduced her to the Blues Power Machine when we were traveling in California a few months earlier. She let me be the car DJ, and I had recently discovered his music. We listened to all his albums during that trip, and she became a fan too.

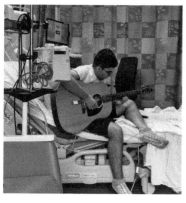

Peter playing his Gibson G45 Acoustic
Photo Credit - Dede Dankelson, 2019

Mom posted the video of me playing and tagged Jared and Mark Agnesi from Gibson in it. Jared is known for playing a Les Paul and even had a signature model made by Epiphone, one of Gibson's brands. I was shocked when Jared reposted the video and sent me a message.

The first thing I did was call Dad to ask him what I should do. He said, "Call Jared!" Really, just dial his number and talk to him? I was more than a little star struck!

When I called Jared, the first thing I said on the phone was, "Sorry I butchered your song." If I had known Mom was going to share that video with the world, I would've done a better job! Just talking to Jared about guitars and his music made my entire night.

He invited me to meet him at an upcoming show in

Chicago where he was opening for John 5, another guitar player I admire. As if that wasn't amazing enough, he asked if I wanted to play a song with him on stage. My head just about exploded with excitement!

Talking to Jared really made me want to get home and start practicing. Dr. Ida liked how I was doing and gave the go ahead for discharge on Friday afternoon. At the beginning of this journey, we were told I would be in the hospital anywhere from three to four weeks. I was home in ten days!!!

Our last night in the hospital, Mom said she needed to use a restaurant gift card. She left me with the nurse call button and my phone while she went out to dinner. I was able to ask for help if I needed it by then, and it was nice to finally be sort of alone for a while. I think Mom needed a break too.

Dad arrived in the morning to pick us up. There isn't anything much better than escaping the hospital walls. We loaded up the car and headed home where I could recover with the things I love most-- my own bed, my guitars, and our dogs.

I've always had a dog to welcome me home from the hospital and this time was no exception. Abby and Dexter loved having our family back together and investigating all the hospital smells. It felt good to be on the couch with them next to me.

I didn't have much energy to play guitar, but I couldn't resist a brief jam session. It was mid-September, and Jared's show in Chicago was less than two months away. I had to start practicing!

Mom didn't hesitate to let me sleep in my own bed that first night home. My jaw wasn't wired shut this time, and I was getting around fine on my own. I don't think I was even taking pain meds anymore.

I love the peace and quiet of my bedroom. I listen to an album almost every night before falling asleep, and it felt so good to be back to that routine. Music is truly my therapy.

I had to fill out one of those forms in elementary school once where you answer questions about what you want to be when you grow up. One of the questions asked, "If you could do anything, what would it be?" I answered, "Sleep."

Mom looked at me kind of funny and said, "No, I don't think you understand the question. If you could travel anywhere, meet anyone, do anything... what would you do?"

"Sleep," I repeated. She rephrased it a few more times, but my answer never changed.

I was probably around eight at the time and had already had multiple hospitalizations and more than twenty surgeries. For me, especially at that time, being home in my room and getting to sleep uninterrupted was heaven. It still is.

I would answer the question differently now because a lifelong dream for me is headlining my own tour. Meeting Angus Young or Slash would also make that list. They are two of my biggest influences and guitar heroes.

I was discharged on September thirteenth and had to come back for an outpatient surgery just six days later. This was expected. Dr. Ida needed to check my airway and make sure the graft was healthy and healing. I call those "stitch and go" procedures, and its usually just Mom with me for those.

She said if I was feeling up for it after the surgery, we could make a stop at Chicago Music Exchange on the way home. I wanted to check out Jared's signature "Old Glory" Epiphone Les Paul. It's all black with a single P90 pickup.

That motivated me to wake up and be discharged ASAP! The surgery was early, and I was out quickly. We had lunch at my favorite post-op pizza place, Gino's East, before heading to Chicago Music Exchange.

Mom posted about my surgery the night before and mentioned we might be stopping by Chicago Music Exchange (CME) on the way home. We received a warm welcome when we got to the store, and they had one of Jared's Epiphone Les Paul's ready for me to try out. The sales manager, Shelby Pollard, also pulled out vintage guitars from their vault, including the infamous Scarface. If you know... YOU KNOW!

It was incredible getting to hold and play those guitars. CME is my version of a kid in a candy store! Mom kept having to leave and put more money in the parking meter. When she finally got me headed toward the door, Shelby said, "Wait. You forgot this." He handed me Jared's Epiphone Les Paul and said it was a gift from Chicago Music Exchange.

Peter at Chicago Music Exchange with the Jared James Nichols Signature Epiphone Les Paul "Old Glory"
Photo Credit - Dede Dankelson, 2019

As if getting the VIP treatment wasn't enough to make the day special, I now had a beautiful guitar. Receiving so much kindness motivates me to stay positive and pay it forward. A day that started out with surgery ended with a heartful of gratitude and a new guitar.

Three weeks later I was back in the operating room at Lurie's for another "stitch and go." The trachea graft still looked healthy and was healing well. So well, in fact, that Dr. Ida said he no longer needed to do these follow up bronchoscopies. Mom was, of course, happy to hear that. But her plan had been to coordinate closure of the g-tube site with one of the follow-up scopes.

I didn't care, I was thrilled with this news and ready for a celebratory stop at Chicago Music Exchange on our way home from the hospital. Mom obliged, and we met CME's General Manager, Pete Falknor, at the store that day. He knew I was playing with Jared soon and asked if I'd like to borrow a guitar and amp to play at the show. Ummmm..... YEAH!

The day of the show, we stopped at CME where I borrowed a new 1960s Standard Les Paul and a Marshall amplifier. We then went to Reggie's for sound check and dinner with the band.

What an epic night for all of us. Shelby and Peter from CME came out to watch me play, and I'm pretty sure I saw a tear in Mom's eye. To see me on stage after being on a ventilator just eight weeks earlier had to be emotional for my parents.

Jared and his band, Dennis Holm on drums, and Barron Fox on bass, were so fun to jam with. The crowd was incredible and even chanted my name. When my song was done, I enjoyed the rest of the set and the John 5 concert from the balcony. What an incredible show!

The energy from that night kept me going strong to face

Peter at Reggie's with Jared James Nichols, Dennis Holm, and Barron Fox
Photo Credit - Dede Dankelson, 2019

one last surgery in 2019. Mom was not giving up on the plan to close my g-tube site. It was November, and I had met all deductibles. She wanted that surgery in the books by year end. Thanks a lot Mom! I just had four surgeries in two months, and she was rallying for the next one.

First, we needed a consult with pediatric surgery to discuss options. The quickest appointment we could get was with a nurse practitioner. She presented us with two options: removing the tube and waiting to see if it closed on its own, or surgically closing the stoma (hole). Sound familiar? Same options I had for the trach stoma closure.

The idea of removing the tube and having stomach acid leaking on my skin was not appealing at all. After nineteen years, none of us were hopeful the stoma would close on its own. I was also concerned about how it would interfere with playing guitar. So, I once again chose the more difficult option. It's what felt best for me, and I wanted nothing to interfere with my guitar playing.

The first available surgery date was November twenty-first. It seemed like a good sign, as that was the eighteen-year anniversary of when Uncle Justin became my guardian angel. Mom knew he'd look out for me in this final surgery that would literally bring closure to my lifelong medical goals.

Mom and I headed to the hospital on November 21, 2019 for my thirty-fifth surgery. It was scheduled for one thirty in the afternoon, which meant no eating the entire day. Afternoon surgeries can also be prone to delays if earlier cases go long or a trauma case comes in. That day was no exception.

We waited in pre-op for nearly six hours, and we were both going crazy in that small, curtained space. I was starving and Mom kept stepping out to grab a sip of water. She felt bad eating or drinking anything in front of me.

I was worried she was going to yell at someone and make things worse for me. She knew there was nothing we could do but wait it out though. I think knowing this was the end of the line for at least the indefinite future made it a tad more tolerable despite our misery.

We knew I'd be spending the night for observation, so it was either wait in pre-op or wait in a room. Still, the waiting was making my anxiety worse. As the hours went by, I eventually got some anti-anxiety medication, so that was entertaining for Mom.

Jared James Nichols and his drummer, Dennis Holm, called me on FaceTime before their show that night. Mom later asked me if I remembered talking to them, but it was only a hazy memory. I checked my phone after she mentioned that because I also had a blurry recollection of sending some goofy texts!

The surgery was about two hours, and everything went very well. I had more pain this time and spent a restless night in the hospital. Compared to everything else I've been through; I didn't expect this to be a difficult recovery. I didn't consider they would be cutting through stomach muscle though.

Mom hadn't thought about it being painful either. She had a c-section with my brother and said it was probably a similar healing process. I was bent over for a few weeks, and it did make playing guitar difficult.

While that recovery was more painful than anticipated, it was my last surgery. Well, at least that we know about! I'm experienced enough to realize there will always be potential surgeries in my future, but I don't have any definite ones hanging over my head anymore.

It was nice to celebrate the holidays and wind down 2019 with all of that behind me. My only continued dilemma was learning how to sneeze. The first time I sneezed after closing the hole in my neck totally freaked me out! Mom was like, "What was that?!"

Air flows through the path of least resistance, and, for me, it always went through the hole in my neck (trach stoma). Without the opening, air was forced through my mouth and nose. I made crazy sounds and hurt myself every time I felt a sneeze coming on. This especially hurt when I was recovering from the g-tube surgery.

I've finally figured out that the words "Ah-Choo" actually mean something. The air blows out your mouth when you say that. Who knew?!

Other than a few weird situations like sneezing, my body adjusted well to losing the third airway source. I sleep well with the CPAP and don't mind using it because I'm getting the best sleep I've had in years. My only complaint would be the inconvenience of traveling with it, especially when flying.

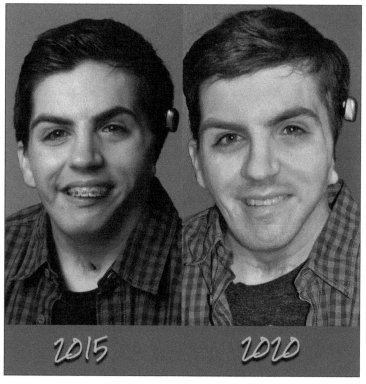

Peter before and after jaw surgery and trach stoma closure
Photo Credit - Dede Dankelson, 2015 and 2020

SEVEN

Amplifying Positivity

With no surgeries on the horizon, I kicked off 2020 ready to rock my life. For the first time since we started speaking, I was able to travel and be flexible with my schedule. Until this time we couldn't travel far or be gone too long because I had to keep up with my own schoolwork.

We had engagements in January and February, then traveled to California in March. The Orange County trip was our fifth consecutive year speaking with sixth graders in the Capistrano Unified School District on behalf of Children's Craniofacial Association (CCA). We were more than happy to escape the Chicago winter and once again donate our time.

One of the families we've met through CCA lives in the school district, and they've always welcomed us into their home for the week. Gibson also supported our message, thanks to our connection with Mark Agnesi. They loaned me a Flying-V guitar and Mesa Boogie amplifier to play at the schools. That was a big hit with both me and the students.

Mom and I drove to the Gibson showroom in Los Angeles to pick up the gear, and it was great to meet the L.A. staff.

(left) Peter with the Gibson Flying V (center) Dede and Peter on the Gibson Guitar of Thrones (right) Peter with Norman Harris on AGN
Photo Credit - Dede Dankelson and Trey Ewald (Gibson), 2020

Such a cool place! They had the new Slash guitar collection there, so I got to admire those beauties.

Mom wanted a pic on the *Guitar of Thrones*, which is a replica made to resemble the throne used in the series *Game of Thrones*. She and Dad were big fans of the show. Gibson's throne is created from one hundred original guitars and is usually on display at the showroom and trade shows.

I couldn't be in L.A. and not visit Norman's Rare Guitars again. Mom didn't hesitate this time. We had only been there once before, but the staff already felt like family.

I did another interview with Norm, and I got to jam with Michael Lemmo. Lemmo is a world-class guitar player who took over as manager of Norman's Rare Guitars when Mark Agnesi left for Gibson. As always, the entire staff at Norm's was welcoming, and we enjoyed our time at the store.

I also did an interview with Norm for All Guitar Network (AGN). AGN is an online music community that produces

Peter with Michael Lemmo at Norman's Rare Guitars
Photo Credit - Dede Dankelson, 2020

stories and interviews with guitar players. They have a studio set up next to Norman's Rare Guitar shop.

Mom eventually pulled me out of my guitar dream. She had plans to visit the new Benheart USA boutique in Beverly Hills. Dad told me to keep an eye on her wallet. He knew she wanted to check out the bags and was nervous about her going into the shop unchaperoned!

The California store is owned by Katherine Kelly Lang and Dominic Zoida. Mom had been messaging them on Instagram, and they knew we had purchased a jacket and met Ben in Florence. Walking into the Beverly Hills store was like returning to Florence. It had the same look, feel, and leathery smell.

Dom and Kelly love giving customers the authentic Benheart experience. They've been trained on how to brand items with your name and make custom belts. Mom was in shopping heaven, and I knew Dad was in trouble!

I couldn't keep a close eye on Mom though because Richard Fortus came into the store while we were there! He's a guitarist for Guns N' Roses, and I was thrilled to talk all things AC/DC and GNR with him.

Fortus is also a huge AC/DC fan. I loved hearing stories from his perspective, like when he watched Axl Rose audition for AC/DC. Fortus is who got me interested in listening to Paul Kosoff, guitarist for the band, Free. He said that Angus Young was a Kosoff fan and that you can hear the influence in Angus' playing.

I did eventually get Mom out of the store, but not before she purchased a bag (or two—sorry Dad). Before we left, Kelly invited us to visit CBS Studios. She's portrayed the role of Brooke Logan on *The Bold and the Beautiful*

Peter with Richard Fortus at Benheart USA in Beverly Hills
Photo Credit - Dede Dankelson, 2020

Dede and Peter with Katherine Kelly Lang on the CBS Set of The Bold and The Beautiful
Photo Credit - Unknown, 2020

for over thirty years. It was fun to be on set, and we enjoyed hanging out in her dressing room with her cute little pup, Rafa.

After visiting the studio, we made the drive back to Orange County to prepare for a week of visiting schools. We had one to two presentations booked every day, and we both loved every minute of it. The students are always so excited and welcoming, and it energizes us. Positive vibes are contagious!

We returned home excited for what the rest of 2020 would bring, including a family trip to Paris and Amsterdam for Spring Break. We had tickets for a Jared James Nichols concert in The Netherlands, and I was more excited about that than seeing the Eiffel Tower!

We also had more speaking visits booked in Montreal, Chicago, and Detroit. It was shaping up to be a great year. But then, you know the rest of 2020's story-- nothing like a global pandemic to rain on your parade.

Like the rest of the world, our vacation plans were cancelled, and we went into lockdown. For Illinois it was three months of no dining out, no in-person school, no haircuts, and so on. Summer wasn't much better with no concerts or festivals.

It was a tough year for everyone, especially musicians and music venues. What I missed most was performing and speaking. Being on stage energizes and motivates me, and it simply can't be duplicated through a screen.

The silver lining during that initial lockdown was social media. Before COVID, our social content was aimed at getting the attention of educators and schools. Mom started our @PetesDiary TikTok Channel in February of 2020, just before we went to California. She saw how the platform was growing, especially with teens.

We got a little engagement on TikTok after the school assemblies, but once quarantine hit, there wasn't much to post. Mom thought we should record something funny about rocking your ear off, so we posted a video of me playing guitar while my prosthetic ear gradually fell off. That got some views!

Interestingly, a lot of the comments were about how good my guitar playing was and not so much about my ear falling off. That motivated me to share a few guitar covers.

The first big surge on TikTok happened when my "Hotel California" guitar solo went viral. It was incredible watching the numbers go up on that video, and it was exciting to get so much engagement. I also started going live on TikTok and had quite a few viewers each time. With the pandemic, I had a lot of extra time to practice and record videos. Learning to play new songs gave me something fun to work on.

With the increased following, came questions about the device on my head, so I recorded a video about my hearing aid explaining how it worked and that I had a magnet implanted in my head. That video also went viral, which made me proud. I believe that talking about my condition in a confident but humorous way encourages people to be more accepting of anyone who looks or feels different.

One of the best moments was when a younger boy with the same type of hearing aid duetted my TikTok video. He captioned it, "finally found someone like me." For me, that's what social media and motivational speaking is all about--encouraging others to embrace their own differences and feel less alone.

I received hundreds of messages from followers who could relate to having a physical difference. They said that finding the @PetesDiary TikTok account made them feel better about themselves. This is exactly what I hope for in sharing both my story and guitar playing. Pete's Diary social channels will always be one hundred percent positive and encouraging.

When Instagram introduced Reels, Mom experimented by posting some of my guitar covers from TikTok. Once again, we were successful at getting engagement and gained thousands of new followers. It was exciting to finally see our social media reaching more people.

Social Media Comments, 2020

Producing new content, writing, and scheduling posts is a lot of work. If you have a small following with little engagement, it's challenging to stay motivated. You don't feel like anyone is reading or watching what you create.

Mom had been working at building our social following for over two years, ever since we made Pete's Diary into an LLC. She was getting frustrated with the lack of engagement and daily grind of putting out content. We were grateful to finally be making an impact.

This new following encouraged us to transition our target audience from educators to music enthusiasts. We integrated the Pete's Diary mission of amplifying positivity and self-acceptance with the music and guitar covers. It's been a home run!

With so much isolation and negative energy on social media, people are drawn to posts like ours that make them feel better. We also engage with our followers as much as we can because we want Pete's Diary to be more than an account you follow. We want our channels to feel like a community that shares a love of music and positive energy.

One of our first weekly posts was #WednesdayWisdom where Mom shares a guitar video and motivational tip that plays off the song title. For example, "Sometimes you have to run with the devil before you can appreciate an angel" was posted with my cover of Van Halen's "Runnin' with the Devil." Or, "When the world closes in on you like the Hotel California, grab a guitar and crank the amp up to 11" was posted with my cover of The Eagles' "Hotel California."

During the initial lockdown we started *The Pete's Diary Show* where we talked about music, motivation, and kindness. I think we did about ten episodes before Mom decided she didn't want to be in front of the camera anymore. Quarantine was seriously getting to her. She wasn't motivated to put on makeup and real clothes for the videos!

Mom thought we should replace *The Pete's Diary Show* with a new series of me talking about a band or favorite guitarist. She knew I had acquired a lot of knowledge about the artists I'm drawn to, and she believed our followers would enjoy hearing my thoughts. The series was called *Pete's Playlist*, and it aired weekly on our IGTV and YouTube channels for over twenty weeks.

As the pandemic went on, we continued merging the motivational content with my guitar videos. I also posted about my life with Goldenhar Syndrome, usually with a sprinkle of humor mixed in. Music and laughter, we believe, are universal connectors that bring people together. Those two things will always be part of our content.

The biggest compliment I get on social media is when kids with differences follow and look up to me. It's an incredible honor to be someone's mentor. Another favorite comment is from followers who have started playing guitar after watching my videos. I love that I'm helping people find comfort in music. It's what helped get me through some of my toughest recoveries, so I know it works.

Messages from all ages tell us that what we're doing is making a positive impact. I've received some incredible gifts from followers. Two in particular stand out. Corey duBrowa found @Petes_Diary on Twitter and loved our content. He emailed Mom shortly after my twentieth birthday asking if he could send a belated gift.

Corey said he had a few vintage guitars sitting in a storage unit. He wanted to send one of them to me and asked my parents for recommendations. Boy, was I surprised when a 1978 Buttercream Fender Stratocaster showed up at our door. What a beautiful guitar!

The guitar brings me joy every day, but it also brings joy to anyone who hears the story. Sharing Corey's random act

1978 Fender Stratocaster sent to Peter from Corey duBrowa
Photo Credit - Dede Dankelson, 2020

of kindness with our followers uplifted a lot of hearts. I love it when stories like this get attention. They mute the overwhelming amount of negativity we consume on social media.

Shortly after receiving the Stratocaster from Corey, Mom was contacted by another fan. Darren Fields knew I was a huge AC/DC fan. He wanted to send me a collectible guitar that was autographed by AC/DC! Mom helped organize this surprise too, and, once again, the positivity rippled through our social channels.

I've received many other thoughtful and kind gifts from fans who want to show their appreciation. Pete's Diary was even voted one of 2020's Best Online Guitar Personalities by Music Radar. We're not sure how we made that list, but it's very humbling to be included with such a talented group of artists. It encouraged both me and Mom to keep amplifying positivity and self-acceptance through music. The world needed it as we all waited for a COVID vaccine.

As 2020 turned into 2021, I continued learning covers and sharing them on social media. I also began writing my own music and looking for a band. Live gigs were cancelled due to the pandemic, so musicians were stuck at home and looking for connections on social media.

That's how Ryan "Rocky" Johnson and I started getting together. I knew Ryan from when he was a drum instructor at School of Rock Libertyville. Ryan played in local cover bands, but COVID had shut them all down. He was looking for someone to jam with, so I invited him over.

Peter with the AC/DC autographed collectible from Darren Fields
Photo Credit - Dede Dankelson, 2020

We began hanging out, and I shared some of my riffs. He started adding drum tracks, and we eventually had three to four songs in various stages of completion. At the same time, I was taking an online songwriting class and had written a bluesy, acoustic song called "Can't Stop Staring." Ryan recorded and mixed it for me. That's how my first single was released.

"Can't Stop Staring" is about living with microtia (missing ear) and the inevitable staring. It's a fun quirky song and my first attempt at singing. I'd never been interested in vocals, but my parents pushed me to take lessons. They believed I should develop my voice if I wanted to be a professional musician.

That was the dilemma Ryan and I faced as we worked to finish our songs. Who was lead vocals? Who would play bass? Finding a singer that fit the rock & roll songs we were writing was essential. I felt that my voice was good for Blues and backup vocals but not the right fit for what we wanted to create. Enter Mac McRae.

I played in School of Rock Libertyville's House Band with Mac for about a year before I aged out. Mac is a great guitar player and performer. He also had the voice we were looking for. Our only hesitation with bringing Mac on board was his younger age. Mac's just fifteen and still in high school. Age, however, isn't as impor-

Peter, Ryan Johnson & Mac McRae
Photo Credit - Dede Dankelson, 2021

tant as talent, and the difference fades away when the three of us are on stage.

Mac was so excited to join us that I convinced him to play bass. That gave us everything we needed to move forward. Together we're *The Peter Dankelson Trio* or *PD3*. We each loved the idea of being a trio, and we're having a blast working together.

Friend and singer/songwriter, Trapper Schoepp, is mentoring us through the writing process and producing our first album. Trapper, you may recall, is a connection I made through my work with Harmony 4 Hope.

Our target is to release the album in Spring 2022, but I'm learning a lot needs to get done before that happens. It's been difficult finding time to work together, but we're enjoying the process. I'm most excited about getting into the studio to record.

We can't wait to share the songs with Pete's Diary fans. I've posted a few teaser videos, and the response has been very positive. Once we're done recording, I'll be able to focus on building excitement for the release. I'm looking forward to offering our fans something more than videos of cover songs. It's going to feel like a "thank you" for how supportive they've been.

The connections I've made on social media have led to some fun opportunities. Earache Records, a UK label, reached out to me in Spring 2021 about promoting one of their new bands. They sent a pre-release link and asked me to give *Mojo Skyline* by The Dust Coda (TDC) a listen. I enjoyed it and posted a video playing one of their songs.

I love that I can introduce new music to my followers while also helping bands get exposure. It's a win for everyone. After TDC's album release, I did a few more collaborations with them, including an AC/DC cover of T.N.T. with their lead singer, John Drake.

Earache Records reached out to me a few months later about promoting another album release. This time it was *Hellbound* by Buckcherry. I listened to the album and posted a cover of the title track to promote it. That led to an invitation to meet the band at one of Buckcherry's concerts.

Mom looked through their tour dates and asked if we

could meet them at Summerfest in Milwaukee. The week of the show, Stevie Dacanay reached out and invited me to not only meet the band, but to also play "Hellbound" with them on stage! Oh, HECK YEAH!!!!

I hadn't had an opportunity to perform for that big of a crowd in nearly two years. Stevie D. is one of Buckcherry's guitarists, and it was such an honor being invited to play with him. He said they were giving me an extended solo during the song. I was pumped and had only a few days to practice.

The concert at Summerfest was amazing. I loved being backstage. Billy Rowe, Buckcherry's other guitarist, talked to me quite a while after the show about Australian bands and players that influenced AC/DC's Angus and Malcolm Young. I love learning about the influences of other guitarists. It reveals so much about their playing style.

Peter with Buckcherry at Summerfest in Milwaukee
Photo Credit - Buckcherry, 2021

Performing with Buckcherry was a great experience. I know it's not easy to invite a guest to play in the set, and I really appreciate that they did that for me. We shared professional video from the show, and it totally amplified positive vibes on our social channels. It's yet another example of the impact an act of kindness makes.

Social media exposure has also given me the opportunity to play with Chicago Blues Hall of Famers like Linsey Alexander and Mary Lane. They've welcomed me into the Chicago music scene, and it's an honor to play with their bands.

Linsey plays a Gibson 339. I had been shopping for a hollow body guitar but most of the body styles were too large for me. Linsey let me play his 339 a few times and offered to sell it to me. The 339s are difficult to find. Guitar shops don't stock many since most players prefer the larger 335 body style. Mom and Dad surprised me when they bought the guitar from Linsey as a Christmas gift. Linsey even signed it for me!

Peter with Linsey Alexander
Photo Credit - Dede Dankelson, 2020

Al DiMeola is another musician who reached out to me on social media. He found the @Petes.Diary Instagram account and enjoyed my videos. He knew I had hearing loss since birth and wanted to make sure I was protecting what I had. Mr.

DiMeola knows from personal experience how long-term exposure to loud music causes hearing loss or problems like tinnitus (ringing in the ear). I'm working from half of what most people have already, so I need to be extra diligent about wearing hearing protection.

Mom and Dad took me to one of Al DiMeola's shows, and I was blown away by his playing. I have so much respect for the skill of jazz players, and Al DiMeola is one of the best. His show was unbelievable, and it was an honor to meet him backstage after the concert. I loved talking to him about music and his playing style.

Peter backstage with Al DiMeola
Photo Credit - Dede Dankelson, 2021

Social media connections have also provided interview opportunities to share my story. One of those was on a podcast called Brand Retro with host Mike Brevik. Mike is also the owner of Cyberdogz Marketing, and he volunteered to create a professional logo for us.

We've used the new Pete's Diary logo to set up an online store with fun products for our fans. It's been exciting to learn that our social followers live all over the world. We shipped one of our shirts all the way to South Africa! How cool is that?

Mom and I are looking forward to the return of speaking engagements. That was our main source of revenue prior to COVID. We've done a few virtual presentations over the last year, but it's not as enjoyable. I need the energy of an in-person audience. It's challenging to gage reactions and feel connected over Zoom.

I'm looking forward to traveling for both speaking and playing gigs. Mom and I have a new presentation that includes some of my original music along with parts of my story that inspire audiences to live a positive life of purpose. Think of it as a TED Talk that ROCKS!

As far as my medical journey, the future is always unpredictable. As of this writing, I don't require any further surgeries. I may need procedures to help with my vision, hearing, or airway, but only if complications arise. I could have elective surgeries like external ear reconstruction, but they don't interest me at this time in my life. The only one I briefly considered was surgery on my hypoplastic thumb.

I'm missing muscle in my left thumb, which is my fretting hand. There is a surgery where muscle can be taken from an-

Peter's left hypoplastic thumb
Photo Credit - Dede Dankelson, 2021

other part of my body and grafted to my hand. This would give me a functional thumb.

While the idea is appealing, it would mean months of occupational therapy and not being able to play guitar for several weeks. It's not a risk I'm willing to take, and I'm used to playing without my thumb.

As an adult, I have annual check-ups for my hearing, vision, kidney function, and neck stability. I still don't eat much solid food. I have lingering sensory issues and don't derive any pleasure from eating. Many textures, flavors, and temperatures are unsavory to me. I consume food merely to sustain myself, mostly from liquid shakes.

My family remains involved with both Children's Craniofacial Association and Harmony 4 Hope charities. Mom is on the board of directors for both non-profits, and I often speak on their behalf. CCA's annual retreats were virtual for 2020 and 2021, and we are excited to reconnect in person for 2022.

I hope this glimpse into my first act helps you see that circumstances don't define your life. We all go through good and bad times. We all experience anxiety and excitement. It's how you choose to manage those events and emotions that makes you either a hero or a victim in your story.

Living with Goldenhar Syndrome is difficult, but it's not all bad. It's given me opportunities that I wouldn't have otherwise. I would've never met Coach Babcock and been inspired to be a difference maker. That simple mantra has shaped my life as much as Goldenhar Syndrome.

Being a difference maker means I choose not to dwell on the past. I strive to give my best performance every day, and I make the most of every stage life presents—even pandemics.

EIGHT

How I Stay Positive

As I said in the beginning, my story is about choices. Some choices, like playing guitar, are of my choosing. I wake up every day and choose to keep playing, no matter what. It's an easy choice because I love it so much.

Other choices are difficult. Choosing to embrace Golden-har Syndrome and make the most of circumstances I can't control is hard. Growing up, my parents often told me, "You can always find someone better off than you, and you can always find someone worse off than you. It doesn't mean that what you're dealing with isn't scary or painful. It just means that it's relative to your own experience."

Saying this validated how I was feeling about an upcoming surgery. It also reminded me that I wasn't the only person fighting a difficult battle. Everyone faces adversity. I had more than some but less than others. Viewing my challenges in this way made me look at my life from a perspective of gratitude, not self-pity.

That gratitude helps me stay positive during tough times. It generates positive self-talk that builds mental grit. You know that little voice inside your head? It can either build you up or tear you down.

That's why the words we use to describe ourselves are so important. They shape how we feel about ourselves and our life. Self-acceptance is a lifelong practice. It's something you must choose to work at every day.

I like to think of my life as a book full of blank pages. Every day is an opportunity for me to focus on what I want to write about the most. I think the most about guitars, so that's my biggest chapter right now! We all have chapters we'd like to tear out, and we all have a limited number of pages.

You control how long a chapter is by how much time you invest thinking about it. It's never too late to shorten some chapters and focus more on others. You do this by editing your thoughts.

Editing is also a lifelong process. You must shorten chapters to make room for new ones. You must limit the impact of some characters to add new ones. You must rewrite chapter titles to reflect how you perceive your life. It's constantly changing.

Goldenhar Syndrome, for example, used to be a scary chapter in my book. I thought about my birth story in titles like *Premature and Deformed* and *Born with Birth Defects*. They are both true. Those words didn't make me feel very good about myself though.

As I grew up and reflected more on my birth, I no longer felt that way. I wanted a more positive, empowering title. Now I think about my birth title as, *Baby, I was Born This Way* (credit to Lady Gaga for writing this powerful song). I like this title because those words make me feel good about myself.

Another chapter I write differently is about my missing ear. I used to think of it as, *Missing an Ear is Weird*. That may be true, but, again, those words didn't make me feel very good. Plus, it didn't express how much fun I have pranking people with the prosthetic. I prefer the title, *Why It's Fun to Have Fake Body Parts!*

Peter having fun with his prosthetic ear
Photo Credit - Peter Dankelson, 2019

Something else that impacts your life is the overall title of your book. The title of your book reflects how you choose to live your life. Do you think of yourself as the victim or as the hero in your story?

I could title my life story, *What It's Like to Suffer from Goldenhar Syndrome*. That title says I think of myself as a victim. It makes me think that everything that happens in my life is about Goldenhar Syndrome.

That's not true. I'm more than a medical condition. I want my story to reflect my entire life, including my sense of humor and love of music. The title of my book is *Rocking My Life as a Metal Head*. Get it? I literally have a head full of metal, and I like heavy metal music.

That title guides my mental focus every day. It makes me feel good and reminds me that it's okay to laugh once in a while. It inspires me to be positive and purposeful with my life. The title *Rocking My Life* motivates me to make the most of every day.

What's the title of your life story? Do you choose to make the most of every day?

Peter with his Gibson SG and an X-ray showing off his medical hardware
Photo Credit - Doug White Photography, 2021

Afterword

How to be Your Own Hero

Pete's Diary offers the following programs and services to help you live a positive life of purpose.

Motivational Speaking & Concerts

Peter and Dede speak at schools, conferences, and community events. Through a combination of music and storytelling, they will show you how to embrace your differences and build positivity into your life. Peter and his band are also available for concerts, touring, and session work. Direct all inquiries to Dede@PetesDiary.com.

Social Media & Website

Follow Pete's Diary on TikTok (@PetesDiary), Instagram (@Petes.Diary), Twitter (@Petes_Diary), Facebook (@Petes-Diary), and YouTube (Pete's Diary Official).

Contact us through our website at www.PetesDiary.com or email Dede@PetesDiary.com.

Online Courses

Visit www.petesdiary.com/online-courses to download worksheets and instructions.

The Hero's Toolbox
How to build confidence and self-acceptance.

1. Value Yourself: identify your personal values and use them to guide decisions.
2. Practice Gratitude: appreciate what you have.
3. Manage Your Mood: take charge of your emotions.
4. Build Mental Grit: make choices that are in your best interest, even when you're afraid.
5. Find Your Tribe: identify healthy relationships that align with your values and interests.

The Hero's Script
How to live your life with positivity and purpose.

1. Embrace Your Story: own your past and present.
2. Envision Your Future: identify and prioritize your goals.
3. Influence Your Destiny: reconcile your past, present, and future.

Acknowledgements

Thank you and our deepest gratitude to the doctors, nurses, and staff at C.S. Mott Children's Hospital at University of Michigan, Children's Hospital of Michigan at Detroit Medical Center, Children's Hospital St. Louis at BJC Health-Care, NorthShore University Health System, Helen DeVos Children's Hospital, and Ann and Robert H. Lurie Children's Hospital of Chicago. A special shoutout to Child Life Specialists and Music Therapists. You are angels of healing.

Thank you to our tribe at Children's Craniofacial Association who remain an immense blessing to everyone in our family. To Harmony 4 Hope for giving Peter a platform to share his medical story and love of music. To School of Rock Libertyville for igniting Peter's love of performing.

Thank you to Norman's Rare Guitars, Gibson, Benheart, and Chicago Music Exchange for opening your stores and hearts to us. Mark Agnesi, we are grateful for your friendship and encouragement.

Thank you to Jared James Nichols and Stevie Dacanay (Buckcherry) for giving Peter an opportunity to perform on the big stage.

Thank you to the followers who make our social channels a welcoming and positive community. You are the spark that keeps us going.

Thank you to our family, especially Peter's grandparents, for your unconditional love and support. This story would not exist without you in it. A special thanks to Grandma Sharon Brockhaus for navigating Detroit and Chicago traffic so she could be with us for surgeries.

Thank you to Mike Babcock for encouraging pediatric patients like Peter. Coaching Peter to be a difference maker laid the foundation for Pete's Diary. We believe that one act of kindness can change someone's life, and you did that for us.

Peter & Dede

Authors

Peter Dankelson

Peter Dankelson is twenty-one years old and undergone thirty-six surgeries to correct birth defects from Goldenhar Syndrome. He is a musician and motivational speaker for Pete's Diary where his humor and music encourage others to embrace what makes them different. Peter was recognized as one of Music Radar's Top Online Guitar Personalities of 2020. He has been honored as a Champion of Hope and Patient of Courage in the rare disease community.

Dede Dankelson

Dede is the owner of Pete's Diary, which began as a journal she kept after her oldest son, Peter, was born premature with Goldenhar Syndrome. Today Pete's Diary amplifies positivity and self-acceptance through music. Dede serves on the Board of Directors for Children's Craniofacial Association and Harmony 4 Hope. She speaks and writes about pediatric healthcare, parenting, and other social issues. Dede resides in the Chicago suburbs with her husband and two sons.

Dede Dankelson and Peter Dankelson
Photo Credit - Images by Marie Moore, 2020